Understanding
Kant's *Groundwork*

Understanding
Kant's *Groundwork*

Edited by
Steven M. Cahn

Hackett Publishing Company, Inc.
Indianapolis/Cambridge

26 25 24 23   1 2 3 4 5 6 7

For further information, please address
    Hackett Publishing Company, Inc.
    P.O. Box 44937
    Indianapolis, Indiana 46244-0937

    www.hackettpublishing.com

Cover design by E. L. Wilson
Interior design by Laura Clark
Composition by Aptara, Inc.

Library of Congress Control Number: 2022946242

ISBN-13: 978-1-64792-118-7 (pbk.)
ISBN-13: 978-1-64792-119-4 (PDF ebook)

The paper used in this publication meets the minimum requirements of American National Standard for Information Sciences—Permanence of Paper for Printed Library Materials, ANSI Z39.48–1984.
                                ∞

Contents

PREFACE

Immanuel Kant's *Groundwork for the Metaphysics of Morals*, written in German and published in 1785, is widely regarded as one of the most influential works in the history of moral philosophy. Indeed, any student of ethics will soon encounter a translation of the book, although trying to read it is likely to cause bewilderment. What, one may ask, is Kant trying to say?

Certain terms appear frequently in the text: the good will, happiness, duty, hypothetical and categorical imperatives, universal law, ends in themselves, and autonomy. But what do these concepts mean?

If a teacher cannot provide clear answers, students are likely to become frustrated, even dispirited. I even knew of a case in which wrestling unsuccessfully with Kant led a student to give up philosophy altogether.

How can effective instructors explain the central Kantian ideas? This book provides the answers. Here seven highly regarded teachers and scholars of Kant's ethics offer remarkably clear explanations of the most important concepts in the *Groundwork*.

To provide such clarity requires not only philosophical understanding but also pedagogical skill. After all, knowing a subject and knowing how to teach it effectively are quite different. And if the students are beginners, finding ways to lead them to grasp complex subject matter while arousing appreciation for it is never easy. Yet as philosopher Tamar Szabó Gendler, dean of the Faculty of Arts and Science at Yale University, once remarked to me, any subject can be clearly explained if you know how. These seven professors have met this challenge in their classrooms and here offer accounts of key ideas that have helped their students understand the essence of Kant's powerful vision.

I am most grateful to these leading scholars for their participation. I also thank Mary Ann McHugh for her expert polishing of all the essays and the staff at Hackett Publishing Company for the care they always take in producing their books. All citations are from James Ellington's translation titled *Grounding for the Metaphysics of Morals* (Hackett).

I began working with William H. Y. Hackett in the mid-1970s, soon after he founded the company that bears his name, and I believe he would have been greatly pleased with the high level of publishing his successors have maintained. I dedicate this book to his memory and that of his dear wife and editorial partner, Frances Hackett.

1

THE GOOD WILL

Nataliya Palatnik

The main passages relevant to the Good Will in the *Groundwork* can be found in the following sections: Ak. 393–394, Ak. 396–405, Ak. 413–414, Ak. 437–440, and Ak. 444.

---

1. The first section of the *Groundwork for the Metaphysics of Morals* begins with a famous statement: "There is no possibility of thinking of anything at all in the world, or even out of it, which can be regarded as good without qualification, except a *good will*" (Ak. 393). What is a good will? Why start the *Groundwork* by talking about it? And what does it mean to say that a good will is good without qualification? What gives it this special value?

Notice that Kant does not simply tell us what a good will is. This is because he takes it to be a familiar concept. Any ordinary reasonable human being is, in principle, able to distinguish morally good from morally bad actions, good will from bad will. Even if she does not spend much time reflecting on the meaning of this concept, she already holds a good will in the highest esteem and knows that its actions have a special moral worth. As Kant puts it, the concept of a good will "already dwells in the natural sound understanding" of morality (Ak. 397); it belongs to the "moral cognition of ordinary human reason" (Ak. 403). The starting point of the *Groundwork* is this common, pre-philosophical concept of a good will. Kant thinks that we can learn a great deal by reflecting on the kind of value we already ascribe to such a will and on the reason why we do so. If we determine what makes the actions of a good-willed person morally good, and what moves her to act, we will better understand what we ought to do to act morally and why. We will be able to fulfill one of the main tasks of the *Groundwork*—to find the supreme principle of morality (Ak. 392).

2. Kant invites us to consider why we hold a good will in such high esteem—what makes it good without qualification—by drawing our attention to what sets it apart from all other things we generally consider to be, in some respect, good and desirable (Ak. 393). These other goods fall into two main categories: "gifts of nature" and "gifts of fortune." The gifts of nature include natural talents, such as intelligence, wit, judgment, and qualities of temperament, such as courage, resolution, and perseverance. These are natural capacities and predispositions that, for the most part, are not of our own making. Our possession of the gifts of fortune, such as health, power, honor, and wealth, is also essentially dependent on factors outside our control. It is not up to us (or at least not entirely) what environment we grow up in, whether we achieve certain social standing or recognition, or how fortunate we are in various business endeavors, for example.

This is why Kant describes these goods as gifts: they are natural endowments we are born with or fortunate circumstances and opportunities we happen upon. As gifts, they are, in a sense, *given* to us to make use of through our actions. And Kant points out that much depends on whether they are properly used or misused. When put to use by a person of good will, these gifts are rightly considered to be good. But they can become "extremely bad and harmful" (Ak. 393) when they fall into the wrong hands, so to speak—when they are used, or rather misused, by a person whose will is not good.

Take the gifts of nature. A human being may be intelligent, imaginative, loyal, tenacious, or have an inborn talent for mathematics or music. But how she uses these gifts depends on the moral quality of her will. Hence, their value is not unconditional. A talented chemist, for example, may use his gift to create life-saving medications or potent poisons. A gifted musician may spend her life teaching and developing the musical tradition of her people or writing songs praising a dictator. This is why the gifts are good in some, but not in all, circumstances, under some, but not under all, conditions. In other words, they are not good without qualification or unconditionally. We regard them as good only under a certain basic condition—only when they belong to a person of good will.

The same holds even for certain qualities of temperament that are particularly helpful to a good will, such as moderation in emotion and feeling, self-control, and calm deliberativeness, even though these qualities are not mere gifts. They are developed through practical experience, through action and reflection on our choices and conduct. As such, they are at least partly products of our will; they require a certain self-discipline and mastery.[1] Since these qualities typically help a good person to be effective in achieving her goals, they may seem to have unconditional

---

1. For a detailed discussion of this point see Stephen Engstrom, "Kant's Conception of Practical Wisdom," *Kant-Studien* 88 (1997): 16–43.

worth (see Ak. 394). Indeed, a number of ancient Greek and Roman philosophers, including Plato, Epicurus, Cicero, and the Stoics, thought of these qualities as virtues that have unconditional value. Yet Kant wants us to notice that these qualities can also become pernicious if the person who possesses them, the core of her character, is not good. While temperance, self-control, and cool-headed reflection are conducive to a good will, they can also facilitate the work of a bad will. "[T]he coolness of a villain," says Kant, "makes him not only much more dangerous but also immediately more abominable in our eyes than he would have been regarded by us without it" (Ak. 394). If these qualities of temperament had unconditional value, a self-controlled, calm, and clever villain would not be so much more repugnant to us. In fact, we would see him as less objectionable than a hot-headed and foolish evildoer. But we do not.

A clever villain is more abominable in our eyes because we see his effectiveness as a kind of perversion—a *misuse*, or *abuse*, of capacities that should make us effective in performing good and noble actions. The villain relies on qualities that help us to be good practical reasoners to do what is morally *un*reasonable. So, far from being good without qualification, the goodness of these special qualities, like that of the gifts of nature, depends on the goodness of the will that puts them to use. Kant makes essentially the same point about the gifts of fortune. Health, power, riches, honor, and even happiness itself, as the "complete well-being and contentment with one's condition" (Ak. 393), are put to use, directed, and responded to by a person deciding how to lead her life, through her choices and actions. Their goodness depends on whether this person's will is good or bad. Like that of the gifts of nature, the value of the gifts of fortune is conditioned on the presence of a good will.

3. Now, things like power or wealth can clearly be put to evil purposes, so it is easy to see that their value is only conditional. But what about happiness? After all, unlike some of the other goods we mentioned, happiness is valued for its own sake and not as a means to some other end. One can meaningfully ask, for example, "Why do you want to be rich?" but not "Why do you want to be happy?" It is then tempting to think it has a special, perhaps the highest and unconditional value. Indeed, there is a long philosophical tradition of thinking of happiness exactly in this way. But Kant wants us to reject this temptation for two reasons. First, he makes a psychological observation that the gifts of fortune that contribute to happiness, and happiness itself, "can make for pride and often hereby even arrogance, unless there is a good will to correct their influence on the mind" (Ak. 393).

The idea seems to be this: In the absence of a good will, human beings tend to misinterpret their good fortune, be it financial prosperity, social status, influential job, good health, or even a generally comfortable, satisfying life, as something they rightfully deserve; to see their happiness as a reflection of their worthiness to be happy and, in some cases, even come to think of themselves as morally superior to those who are less fortunate. In other words, without the correcting influence of a good will, we are given to unjustified moral self-satisfaction and self-conceit—a kind of corruption of the will, which Kant describes as pride and arrogance.[2] Think, for example, of a CEO who considers his powerful position, wealth, and life of ready access to everything he wishes to be a sign of his worth as a human being, even though he cares little that his employees are poorly paid or that his company benefits from a bloody war.

---

2. See Allen W. Wood, *Kant's Ethical Thought* (Cambridge: Cambridge University Press, 1999), 21–22.

A person whose character is corrupted in this way considers his own well-being to be of supreme value for everyone, treating the interests and ends of others as subordinate to his own. But in a good-willed person, this problematic tendency is thwarted. Unlike a person of bad character, she does not take herself to have exceptional moral worth or demand that others put her happiness above all other concerns. As Kant puts it, a good will corrects the corrupting influence of good fortune on the mind by rectifying "the whole principle of action" (Ak. 393). In deciding what to do and how to lead her life, she does not allow for special treatment or exceptions for herself. Rather, Kant tells us, she acts on principles that are conformable with universal ends—ends that can be regarded as good by every rational and reasonable person.

Second, Kant suggests that if happiness had unconditional value, we would see it as good no matter whose happiness it is. Yet a rational and impartial person could never approve of, or delight in, the sight of a villain enjoying a life of uninterrupted happiness and prosperity. So even happiness must be regarded as good only under certain conditions—only when one who is happy is *worthy* of happiness. And what makes a person worthy of happiness is possession of a good will. Hence, a good will is "the indispensable condition of being even worthy of happiness" (Ak. 393).

Only a good will is good unconditionally, or *absolutely*, because its value is independent of any and all external conditions. It remains the same under all conditions and in all circumstances.[3] In contrast, all the other goods, whether valued as a means or, like happiness, for their own sake, are good only conditionally,

---

3. See John Rawls, *Lectures on the History of Moral Philosophy* (Cambridge, MA: Harvard University Press, 2000), 154–56.

or *relatively*, and the condition of their goodness lies in the presence of a good will.

4. Since the value of a good will remains the same under any and all conditions, it is not derived from anything outside of the good will itself. Rather, a good will has *inner* or *intrinsic* worth. Kant describes it as good *in itself*—as "good *only through its willing*" (emphasis added) and "not because of what it effects or accomplishes, nor because of its fitness to attain some proposed end" (Ak. 394). In claiming that "usefulness or fruitlessness" of a good will can neither add to nor diminish its value (Ak. 394), he stresses that its value lies *solely* in the way a good person chooses to act, in what motivates her actions. In Kantian terms, this means that the value of the good will of such a person lies *solely* in the *principle* on which she acts and not in how effective or successful she is in achieving her purposes.

On the face of it, this claim seems implausible. Would we attribute unconditional value to the will of a person who means well, so to speak, but never or rarely accomplishes anything? Imagine someone who is genuinely pained by the misfortunes of others, wishes them well, and even attempts to help on certain occasions, but is never able to sustain his efforts. Suppose, for example, that this person has a deeply pessimistic outlook on life and does not believe that he can ever succeed in improving anyone's circumstances. So, he tries to help, but half-heartedly, and readily gives up when the going gets tough. Or imagine a similarly "well-meaning" person who does not particularly care whether he actually manages to help or not, thinking that, after all, he tries, and that's what counts. As a result, he rarely, if ever, accomplishes what he wishes to accomplish. Clearly, most people would not think that such a will should be held in particularly high esteem.

Examples like these seem to cast doubt on the claim that a good will's usefulness or fruitlessness cannot affect its value. But Kant is careful to point out that a good-willed person is not merely well-meaning or emotionally sensitive to the needs of others. She does not merely *wish* to act well and does not act half-heartedly. She cares deeply about the effectiveness of her actions, "summoning of all the means in [her] power" (Ak. 394) to make a difference in the world. She is genuinely committed to acting well—doing the right thing for the right reason and achieving her goals. Only *this* kind of will, Kant tells us, has its full value *in itself* and would "like a jewel, still shine by its own light" even if, "by some especially unfortunate fate or by the [miserly] provision of stepmotherly nature, this will should be wholly lacking in the power to accomplish its purpose" (Ak. 394).

We would also misunderstand Kant if we took him to hold that the value of a good person's actions has nothing to do with the goodness of her ends. In fact, a good-willed person cannot set bad ends, although there may be a number of ways in which she may fail to achieve her purposes. This is because, in setting an end for herself, a good-willed person makes it her principle to pursue this end through her own efforts. And since the value of a good will lies in its willing—in the principle on which she acts—the goodness of her willing ensures the goodness of her end. She may overestimate her abilities, fail to foresee all the relevant consequences of her efforts, suffer injury or loss as a result of her action, and the like. However, the fact that her action results in an unhappy outcome neither detracts from its value nor makes her end less worthwhile. For, both the value of her actions and goodness of her ends stem from the goodness of her *willing*— from the *principle* on which she acts.

In this picture, a good will sets limits on the particular ends we may adopt and the means we may take to pursue them. This is why, a good person would think, for example, that it is good to have a well-paid job, but not if it involves destroying the environment or disregarding the rights of others; good to lead a healthy, enjoyable life, but not if it involves letting someone else make important decisions for her; good to avoid financial difficulty, but not by lying on a loan application; and, on Kant's view at least, good to be free of pain, but not by committing suicide.

5. That said, the claim that a good will has such a special value, even if it does not accomplish its purposes and even if its actions lead to unhappy consequences, may still seem puzzling. It is natural to think that a situation in which a good person succeeds in achieving her goals is better than a situation in which she does not or when her actions have unwelcome effects—say, when she tries and fails to save a friend from a house fire or she herself dies in the attempt, leaving her family to grieve. And, in fact, Kant would agree. His point about the inner source of value of a good will does not imply that the outcomes of her actions make no moral difference in the world. Rather, it is intended to show that a good will is the highest, or the *supreme*, condition of everything else we may consider good and desirable. This is why he goes on to describe a good will as "the highest good and the condition of all the rest, even of the desire for happiness" (Ak. 396). It is the highest good in the sense that nothing else is a condition of its value, while the value of every other good, be it health, wealth, meaningful friendships, good judgment, or happiness itself, is conditioned on the presence of a good will through whose actions they are to be pursued and preserved.

Kant also makes an important distinction between the *highest* and the *complete* good. Although a good will is the highest good, it is not "the sole and complete good" (Ak. 396). After all, other conditional goods are rightly valued, provided that they accompany a will that is good. Later, in the *Critique of Practical Reason*, he makes clear that the complete good for a person will comprise not only her good will but also her achievement of conditional goods that constitute happiness, where her worthiness to be happy is the *supreme*, or the *highest*, condition of her happiness (see Ak. 5:110). Insofar as she is happy, her situation is *better* than that of a good person who fails in her endeavors, and the world in which the virtuous lead fully happy and satisfying lives is better, more complete in its goodness, than our present, imperfect world in which they often do not.

If Kant is right, a good will is to be valued "much higher than anything which it might ever bring about merely in order to favor some inclination, or even the sum total of all inclinations" (Ak. 394). By "inclination," Kant generally means the habitual sensible desire for some pleasing object or experience (or desire to avoid something displeasing). Most people have inclinations for self-preservation and companionship, for example. But we may also be inclined to binge on sweet foods, seek attention, avoid conflict at any cost, be fearful of strangers, or have inclinations for loyalty, generosity, compassion, or honor. Kant's point is that the value of a good will is in a category of its own. It is beyond comparison with the relative value of satisfying *any* desire or inclination, whether amiable or not, and even of happiness itself, conceived as the complete satisfaction of *all* desires and inclinations.

6.   We said that what gives a good will its exceptional value is its willing the principle on which it acts. To better understand what this means, we need to consider how a good person wills her actions. What motivates her to act? What guides her choices? Indeed, one of the main tasks of *Groundwork I* is to answer these questions. Once we know the answers, we will know what makes actions morally good and will be able to discover the supreme principle of morality.

Kant takes up this task by focusing on the concept of duty, which he describes as the concept of a good will "with certain subjective restrictions and hindrances" (Ak. 397). These restrictions and hindrances are due to the fact that human beings do not always act as they should. While we are able to act from the motive of duty—do the right thing *because it is right*—we have desires and emotions that may move us in ways that are incompatible with morally good action. We experience morality as a demand, telling us what we *ought* to do, even if doing so goes against our every natural inclination. This is why acting from duty often requires a genuine strength of character.[4]

Kant thinks that exploring what makes such actions special in contrast to other kinds of actions will help to bring out the principle that governs a good will. He is particularly interested in contrasting actions done *from* duty with those where a person does an overtly right thing—acts *in accord with* duty—but is motivated in other ways. He distinguishes two kinds of action that accord with duty: (i) those done from some "selfish purpose"—motivated by an inclination not directed to the action itself but to some further end, and (ii) those done from an "immediate inclination"—a desire directed specifically to the action itself, where a subject has no "selfish purpose" and simply *wants* to perform the action for its own sake (Ak. 397).

---

4. In contrast, a *perfectly* good will has no such limitations. Beings who possess such a will, perhaps God and the angels, by their nature, as it were, always act morally. The concept of duty does not apply to them. So it is a good will under subjective restrictions and hindrances, a good will of a finite rational being (e.g., a human being), that is the subject of Kant's analysis of duty in *Groundwork I.*

7. It is easy to see what separates actions of the first kind (overtly right actions done from some selfish purpose) from similar actions done from duty. To illustrate, Kant asks us to imagine a prudent merchant who (when the competition abounds) does not overcharge inexperienced customers "so that a child may buy from him just as well as everyone else may" (Ak. 397). The prudent merchant does the right thing—he keeps a fixed price for everyone, but only because he thinks that this helps to protect his reputation and that having a good reputation benefits his business. Honesty is the best policy, but only because it is to his advantage. So it is clear that his action does not issue from a good will. He acts in *accord* with duty, but not *from* duty—not because treating his customers honestly is the right thing to do.

Now, consider another, loving merchant who charges his customers equally and fairly out of genuine care for their well-being and not as a means to some further end. We may admire his gentle nature and his caring attitude toward others. But does his action manifest a good will? Does it have true moral worth? Kant's answer would be no. To see why, it helps to look at what Kant says about a similar example, that of a person motivated by sympathy.

While helping those in need whenever possible is a moral duty (a duty of beneficence), many people help others simply out of fellow feeling. They are "so sympathetically constituted," says Kant, "that, without any further motive of vanity or self-interest, they find an inner pleasure in spreading joy around them and can enjoy in the satisfaction of others as their own work." (Ak. 398) Like our loving merchant, such a sympathetic philanthropist has no further motive, no selfish purpose—he helps simply because his sympathy with others arouses in him an immediate desire to help them.

We would be right to praise such a person, applaud his generosity, delight in the results of his work, and encourage such behavior in others. Yet Kant argues that his action lacks moral worth. First, he points out that this action's agreement with duty is merely *accidental* because the philanthropist's sole motivation is his sympathetic inclination. When our inclinations are "fortunately directed" (Ak. 398), the resulting actions are beneficial and deserve praise and encouragement. But the same inclination may also be misdirected. Imagine, for example, that our loving merchant comes to care so much for his customers that he stops charging them altogether, neglecting the needs of his children, or that the philanthropist grows so dejected under the stresses of life that he loses all sympathetic concern for the woes of others. As his sympathetic feeling diminishes, so does his desire to help, and so does his beneficence.

But Kant's main point is that in acting from inclination alone, even an admirable one, such as an inclination for sympathy, honor, or loyalty, a person is not concerned with what he is morally required to do.[5] This is why it is merely an accident that his action accords with duty. In the absence of an interest in the moral rightness of his action, his doing the right thing is merely a matter of moral luck (only due to fortunate circumstances) and not an expression of a good will. In contrast, it is not an accident that a person who acts from duty does the right thing—she chooses her actions precisely because she thinks they are morally right. Simply put, her actions agree with duty because she chooses only those actions that do so agree and *because* they do. And she acts this way whether or not she *also* has desires and

---

5. Barbara Herman, "On the Value of Acting from the Motive of Duty," chap. 1, in *The Practice of Moral Judgment* (Cambridge, MA: Harvard University Press, 1993), 4–5.

inclinations that favor the right action or oppose it. This is why her actions manifest a good will. We now understand why Kant claims that the action of our first sympathetic philanthropist lacks moral worth. The moral rightness of helping others in need is not part of his motivation. He chooses to help *only* because he wants to and not because he thinks that helping is morally required.[6] In Kant's terms, the principle on which he acts, the maxim of his action, "lacks the moral content of an action done not from inclination but from duty" (Ak. 398).

8. Now, Kant also imagines two other characters—a dejected philanthropist who, despite losing all sympathetic feeling, continues to lend a helping hand to others in distress, and a stoic one who helps even though he does not have a compassionate nature to begin with. Each of these men acts from duty and not from inclination, and that, Kant stresses, is what gives their actions true moral worth. Kant uses these examples to exhibit duty in its pure form. They should not be taken to imply that a good-willed person always acts contrary to her inclinations, or that she must be cold and indifferent, or be moved *solely* by duty. She may be sympathetic, loyal, generous, and want her business to succeed. But she does the right thing whether or not her inclinations happen to agree with what duty requires. In acting from duty, she acts on a principle that, in a sense, subordinates her desires and inclinations to the moral interest—interest in doing what is morally right, regardless of inclinations or expected outcomes. She helps because, in the first place, she sees her action as something she is morally required to do; she sees it as an unconditional moral

6. Christine Korsgaard, "Kant's Analysis of Obligation: The Argument of *Groundwork I*," chap. 2, in *Creating the Kingdom of Ends* (Cambridge: Cambridge University Press, 1996), 55–57.

requirement—a kind of law for her will. What Kant's analysis of the concept of a good will aims to make clear is that a good-willed person acts from duty and not from inclination, and that she is moved by the very thought that the action is something she is morally required to do, or by what he describes as "respect for the law" (e.g., Ak. 400). It is this special motivation—the respect for the law—that makes her actions morally good.

Given what we now know about acting from duty, we can see that the principle on which a good-willed person acts cannot be based on any inclinations or any effects she may expect from her actions. If so, what is left to guide and motivate her action? Kant's answer is that a good-willed person is motivated by the thought that her maxim has the *form* of the law—that it is *fit* to serve as a universal law. In other words, the principle that governs her will is the categorical imperative, which requires her to act only on that maxim that she can at the same time will as a universal law—as something that everyone wills.

2

HAPPINESS

Anne Margaret Baxley

The main passages relevant to Happiness in the *Groundwork* can be found in the following sections: Ak. 393–394, Ak. 395–396, Ak. 399, Ak. 401, Ak. 405, Ak. 410, Ak. 416, Ak. 418–419, Ak. 423, Ak. 430, Ak. 439, Ak. 441–442, Ak. 444, and Ak. 450.

Kant characterizes happiness as the satisfaction of desires; in other words, getting what we want. To use my own example, Henry might find happiness by drinking Negronis, watching Fellini films, listening to Mozart, reading Nietzsche, writing poetry, vacationing in Rome, and celebrating with family and friends. Further, his satisfaction should be enduring. As Kant notes, happiness is "a maximum of well-being in my present condition and in every future condition" (Ak. 418).

Given that the content of happiness will vary from person to person, what makes Henry happy might conflict with what makes Hannah happy, for she might want entirely different things than he does. And what she wants is up to her. Thus criminals, scoundrels, and villains are just as capable of happiness as anyone else because their happiness amounts to satisfying whatever desires they happen to have. For Kant, therefore, being happy is compatible with being morally bad.

Indeed, Kant holds that happiness is inherently a nonmoral goal that we have based on natural instinct, not reason. Our innate desire for happiness directs us to seek the satisfaction of our inclinations and improve our well-being, a goal Kant sees as our primary non-*moral* purpose in life. Morality, by contrast, directs us to cultivate a good will and abide by the moral law. Happiness and morality need not coincide because morality teaches us how to become worthy of happiness, but not how to be happy (Ak. 393, 442, 450). In brief, for Kant, happiness is a prudential concept, signifying that a person has achieved the things she wants most out of life and done so over time.

Happiness is the one goal of all human beings. Yet we cannot form a definite conception of what would make us happy, for we cannot specify with confidence all our present and future desires. No one knows enough to obtain such knowledge, for it requires omniscience which we do not possess. For this reason, Kant proclaims that "the problem of determining certainly and universally" just what will make a person happy is "completely insoluble" (Ak. 418).

Furthermore, we sometimes have incompatible desires, as when Hannah thinks she wants to be a poet but also seeks luxuries obtainable only by wealth. In such cases, the most important desires for happiness might not be obvious. Other times, what we think will make us happy in the moment conflicts with our long-term satisfaction. Kant gives the example of the agent suffering from gout who finds pleasure in eating the rich foods readily available on the table, even though indulging is bad for his health and will likely diminish his overall happiness (Ak. 399). Moreover, most of us have had the experience of finding that what we thought would make us happy turned out to be a source of discontent. Imagine that, after much reflection, Hannah decides that an opulent lifestyle ultimately matters more than writing poetry. Yet, having succeeded at a job in finance, she finds that she is ultimately dissatisfied.

Kant notes that all the elements of happiness are based on experience, not reason (Ak. 418–419), and thus cannot be known in advance. Kant cites as an example a person who wishes for wealth, superior insight, and long life, only to find that wealth makes her the subject of envy, insight makes her aware of the evils of the world, and a long life turns out to be full of misery (Ak. 418). As a constantly fluctuating ideal of the imagination, happiness remains a somewhat elusive goal that we always wish to attain. However, we can never formulate with certainty a definite recipe for what it would take to be happy.

By stressing that we can only discover what will bring us happiness through experience, Kant notes that happiness is an ideal of the imagination, not a fixed ideal of reason (Ak. 418–419). Reason was given to cultivate a good will, not to seek happiness. Indeed, happiness is not well served by reason, and it gives us "weak insight" in identifying an overall conception of what our happiness looks like and choosing the means for preserving it (Ak. 395–396). Instead, we need to rely on instinct and experience to guide us in our efforts to achieve the satisfaction of the sum of our desires.

Kant realizes the universal need for happiness and includes happiness as part of our complete human good (the highest good, which he defines as virtue plus happiness in proportion to virtue). Nevertheless, he consistently claims that happiness has limited value compared to moral value (Ak. 393, 396). We all naturally seek the satisfaction of the sum of our desires, but happiness, unlike a good will, is not good without qualification. On the contrary, happiness is only morally permissible to pursue when it conforms to duties or moral concerns.

In the *Groundwork*, Kant's main argument in support of the thesis that happiness is a merely conditioned good appears in the context of his discussion of a good will as the only thing good without limitation (Ak. 394–395). Kant tries to show that a good will alone has absolute value by arguing that all other potential goods have limited value in relation to a good will. Kant explains that the various practical and theoretical virtues extolled by his ancient predecessors are not unconditionally good, but good only when combined with a good will. Thus, happiness can produce arrogance in the contented agent unless a good will is present to correct the influence this gift of fortune can have on the mind (Ak. 393). When people enjoy good fortune, they are inclined to suppose that they deserve to be better off, forgetting that happiness depends at least partly on luck. Such arrogance can lead to moral evil. On the other hand, in the morally good agent governed by a good will, the good will limits the agent's pursuit of happiness, ensuring that she acts on her desires only when doing so is permissible (in conformity with duty).

As further proof that happiness is not absolutely good, Kant asserts that an impartial rational spectator can take no pleasure in seeing the vicious person prosper. This point is supposed to remind us that "a good will seems to constitute the indispensable condition of being worthy of happiness" (Ak. 393). The guiding thought motivating Kant's conviction that the agent's happiness is good only when the agent possesses a good will is that a world in which happiness is attained proportionally to virtue is a morally better world than one in which it is not. As Kant sees it, the happiness of the wicked person is morally bad, just as the happiness of the virtuous person is morally good. Thus from the standpoint of reason, justice is served when virtuous people prosper, and vicious people fail to achieve their goals.

As Kant's remarks about the relative value of happiness indicate, he holds that happiness is morally or objectively good only under certain circumstances. By contrast, happiness is not good independently of its relation to other things or an end whose value cannot be defeated by external conditions. Although all human beings consider happiness their primary non-moral end or purpose in life, a person deserves to be happy only on the condition that she possesses a good will and abides by duty, conforming her actions to the moral law. Hence she is justified in pursuing her happiness only on the condition that what she wants does not conflict with duty and moral concerns. In sum, happiness is unequivocally important in a good life, yet it is always eclipsed by morality's supreme value.

A further problem with happiness is that it may conflict with the demands of morality. For example, imagine that Henry wants more than anything else to spend the upcoming summer in Rome, eating his favorite pasta dish of cacio e pepe, visiting with dear Italian friends, and exploring ancient Roman sights. Based on experience, Henry believes another summer in Rome will bring him immense pleasure, and he has spent the better part of a year planning his trip. A difficulty arises, however, when Henry recognizes that he has a conflicting moral obligation to stay home in Scranton to help care for his young niece, whose mother has unexpectedly passed away. From Kant's perspective, circumstances of this sort are unavoidable, for we may find ourselves wanting something that clashes with what we are obligated to do. In these cases, we cannot both abide by duty and act to secure our own happiness. In other words, Kant contends that the demands of morality often restrict, interfere with, or infringe upon our search for personal happiness (Ak. 396, 405, cf. Ak. 442). Thus happiness may be more of a foe than an ally of duty.

Kant offers numerous illustrations in the *Groundwork* of contrary-to-duty actions that may further the agent's own happiness. For instance, the "false promising" example shows that lying might be consistent with our whole future welfare (Ak. 422). Neglecting to develop any of our talents might lead to a life filled with contentment, as Kant imagines in the case of the South Sea Islanders (Ak. 423). In his discussion of the agent who contemplates a maxim of suicide when living would promote more discontent than satisfaction, Kant suggests that suicide might be consistent with advancing our own happiness (Ak. 421–422).

As these illustrations reveal, Kant emphasizes that actions opposed to duty can enhance our happiness, while abiding by duty can diminish our enjoyment of life. He even observes that a morally good person might be unhappy while a vicious person might prosper (Ak. 442, 394).

Yet Kant is adamant that morality always takes priority over the concerns of happiness. Hence we ought to refrain from pursuing happiness when doing so would prevent us from fulfilling our moral obligations. Above all else, we should strive to cultivate a good will, bringing our search for happiness into conformity with duty (Ak. 393).

Happiness is not a moral end but a non-moral goal comprising the maximal satisfaction of empirical desire. Yet the relation between the universal human search for happiness and our moral duties is more complex than this simple statement suggests. To begin with, Kant holds that we have a moral duty to promote the happiness of others (our duty of beneficence). We can be commanded on moral grounds to make the happiness of others our own end because we always want others to help us in circumstances where we need assistance in securing our own welfare

(Ak. 423). Accordingly, by appeal to the universality of reason, it would be contradictory to want others to care about my welfare whenever I need help if I, in turn, never help others when they are in need. Moreover, Kant holds that our moral duty to promote the happiness of others is part of what it means to respect the humanity in others as an end in itself (Ak. 430).

Kant also claims that while we have no *direct* moral obligation to promote our own happiness because what we seek based on inclination cannot be commanded under the name of "duty," our own happiness is *indirectly* a moral duty. In Kant's words:

> To secure one's own happiness is a duty (at least indirectly); for discontent with one's condition under many pressing cares and amid unsatisfied wants might easily become a great temptation to transgress one's duties. (Ak. 399)

This passage from the *Groundwork* appears within a broader discussion of maxims of action that display moral worth. Immediately following the claim that we are indirectly obligated to assure our own happiness on moral grounds, Kant explains that, as a matter of course, all people already have the strongest inclination to promote their own happiness, for happiness is an idea that unites all inclinations. Yet only when we are moved to promote our welfare from duty, not inclination, does our conduct have moral worth. Kant concludes his brief discussion of our indirect duty to our own happiness by stressing that, abstracting from the general inclination to happiness all finite rational agents share, promoting our own happiness from duty is "a law" (Ak. 399).

Readers have rightly puzzled over Kant's surprising remark that happiness, a distinctly non-moral aim we always seek based on instinct, is also the subject of moral duty. How can we make sense of Kant's claim that, apart from the prudential reasons we all share, we have moral reasons for seeking the satisfaction of our desires?

On one plausible reconstruction of Kant's view, he believes that our duty to cultivate a good will by acting in conformity with the moral law directs us to do what we can to overcome temptations to neglect our duties. Kant is especially concerned with the temptation of unhappiness. In other words, feeling unhappy is ultimately bad from a moral perspective because dissatisfaction with our condition can make it more difficult to abide by duty. Thus despite Kant's conviction that we seek happiness without constraint, he thinks that we have moral grounds for pursuing our own welfare as a way to mitigate the moral dangers of unhappiness.

Kant admittedly does not offer any arguments in the *Groundwork* to support the commonsense idea that being unhappy presents a potential obstacle to acting morally. However, in both the *Critique of Practical Reason* and the *Metaphysics of Morals*, he uses the example of poverty to illustrate his basic point. He suggests that the temptation to violate our duty is greater if we are poor rather than wealthy because poverty makes it more likely that we might be tempted to violate the rights of others to secure our own basic needs. Alternatively, consider the examples of Henry and Hannah. Suppose Henry finds himself unhappy after he cancels his plan to spend the upcoming summer in Rome because of a conflicting moral obligation to care for his niece. In that case, the worry is that preoccupation with his feelings of dissatisfaction might lead him to neglect his moral duties. Suppose Hannah is genuinely unhappy with her career in finance and takes no pleasure in the luxuries that she thought she desired. In that case, these are unhappy circumstances that might make it more difficult for her to attend to more pressing moral duties.

Of course, by suggesting that being happy makes it easier to fulfill our duties, Kant does not mean that having our own desires satisfied is *necessary* for abiding by moral demands. That suggestion would indicate that happiness, which Kant takes to be not fully within our control, is a necessary condition of possessing a good will. This idea flouts his thesis that duty alone is sufficient to motivate us to act as morality requires.

In addition, consider Kant's example of the agent who wishes for death, yet despite his own "hopeless sorrow," preserves his life without loving it (Ak. 397–398). This conscientious moral agent is tempted to violate the duty to self-preservation but demonstrates moral strength of will in refraining from taking his own life because he recognizes that morality demands it. We should therefore understand Kant as committed to the more modest proposal that unhappiness is a state of dissatisfaction with our own condition that is problematic from the perspective of morality because lacking happiness *can*, or perhaps *tends to*, make it more difficult to fulfill our duties.

In sum, Kant does not systematically present his views of happiness. On a charitable reading of the *Groundwork*, however, we find that Kant has a coherent theory of happiness, one worth taking seriously. He has a complex account of the nature of happiness for human beings and why we care about it while also offering intriguing views about the potentially corrupting influence of both happiness and unhappiness. He accords happiness a significant role in his broader ethical theory when he insists that it is our primary natural end in life and part of our complete good (our highest good). Moreover, he ultimately sees that happiness has instrumental moral value in mitigating a central temptation to neglect or violate our moral duties and that our own happiness is itself an indirect moral duty. Finally, Kant provides the framework for a plausible account of what a morally good or virtuous agent ought to do in circumstances where she must sacrifice her concerns for happiness for the sake of morality.

3

DUTY

Laura Papish

The main passages relevant to Duty in the *Groundwork* can be found in the following sections: Ak. 389, Ak. 394, Ak. 396–408, Ak. 421–425, Ak. 429–434, and Ak. 439.

In Kant's moral theory, the concept of duty plays a foundational role. While most of us recognize duties, whether obeying traffic rules or helping others, Kant seeks to refine our ordinary beliefs regarding the nature of a duty and the specific duties we should acknowledge.

Kant emphasizes that human beings are conflicted, caring about being morally good but also concerned with their own desires, or what he calls "inclinations." Each person cares deeply about achieving personal happiness, so we all sometimes choose contentment over morality. Thus Kant introduces "the concept of *duty*, which includes that of a good will, though with certain subjective restrictions and hindrances" (Ak. 397).

Kant characterizes duty as "the necessity of an action done out of respect for the law" (Ak. 400), by which he means the

27

moral law. Laws explain how one thing relates to another. In physics, for instance, we find a law according to which the force exerted on an object leads to certain changes in the motion of a moving body; force relates to momentum. In a society with taxation laws, these dictate how the state relates to personal income. The moral law likewise constrains relations but in distinctive ways. Whereas tax laws are contingent and changeable, for Kant, the moral law is necessary and universal. It holds for all rational creatures and specifies how we should interact with others, how we should treat ourselves, and how we should think about the importance of morality. Whereas a law of physics *describes* the world, the moral law *prescribes* how we should act.

The source of the moral law is found within ourselves by the use of pure reason that logically requires we consider the universalizability of our maxims, treat people properly, and thereby act "out of respect" for the moral law (Ak. 400). We thereby act "from duty" (Ak. 403).

To act from duty, we must have a certain mindset and an appreciation of what matters from a moral point of view. Consider, for instance, Kant's example of the business dealer (Ak. 397). If the dealer charges the correct amount even to clueless customers but only because it's good for his reputation, that individual fails to act from duty. Although such an action may look superficially right, the dealer lacks the right motivations. The preoccupation here is neither the humanity of those he does business with nor the universalizability of store policy.

The dealer is an example of someone whose action "accords with duty," but because the morally requisite attitudes are absent, the action is not done "from duty" (Ak. 397). That the dealer is making correct change matches what the moral law instructs us to do, but the motives for complying are drawn exclusively from self-interest. Hence the dealer's actions fail to have what Kant describes as "moral worth" (Ak. 399). While we might nonetheless be glad that the dealer doesn't overcharge anyone, and we might "encourage" the dealer to keep this practice in place (Ak. 398), we have no reason to "esteem" or find "intrinsic worth" in the dealer's actions (Ak. 398, 397). Granted, it would be worse if the dealer acts *neither* in accord with duty *nor* from duty, ripping off folks left and right. Only action done from duty, however, gets Kant's unconditional endorsement.

Note that for Kant, any action done from duty will also be in accord with duty, for duty is concerned with doing the right thing for the right reason, and if we get our reasons right, then our actions will also be right. According to Kant, all human beings have insight into our duties. As he puts it, "I need no far-reaching acuteness to discern what I have to do in order that my will may be morally good" (Ak. 403). We grasp, for example, that no morally worthy action features self-serving lies and that sheer indifference to other people's needs is incompatible with a recognition of their humanity. If we see someone acting in these ways, we can affirm that this person does not respect the moral law and is not acting from duty.

Although critically important, the question of whether someone is acting from duty cannot be answered with confidence. The motives of others are not transparent to us. Indeed, Kant believes we can never even be certain about our *own* motives. "We like to flatter ourselves with the false claim to a more noble motive," and as a result, we may take ourselves to act from duty when, in fact, "some secret impulse of self-love" is governing our motives (Ak. 407). As long as self-interest and the moral law recommend the same actions, we may never be forced to confront whether our self-interest or morality has priority. Acting from duty is, for Kant, "the highest practical function" for all human beings

(Ak. 396). Yet, our conceit and the likelihood of hidden motivations imply that no one can secure bragging rights about having acted from good will.

So far, most will agree with Kant's discussion. Like Kant, we all want to be surrounded by people who not only do the right thing but do it for the right reason. We are also apt to accept Kant's claim that self-deception hampers our efforts to know whether we have acted from duty. Moreover, Kant is likely to find us agreeing with two additional points.

First, even if our actions do not achieve our purposes, they may nevertheless be done from duty. As Kant puts it, moral worth depends "not on the realization of the object of the action, but merely on the principle of volition according to which . . . the action has been done" (Ak. 399–400).

Now, this isn't to say that a person who aims to act in a morally worthy way is inattentive to the consequences of their actions. A conscientious individual hopes for success and will recalibrate as needed; nevertheless, the moral worth of those actions does not depend on what this person materially "effects or accomplishes" (Ak. 394). In short, intentions, not consequences, give an action its moral worth.

Second, we will probably end up agreeing with Kant that actions from duty are actions done from "respect" for the moral law. He wants to highlight how the moral law elicits a distinctive feeling of respect that has both a positive, elevating quality and a negative, painful quality. Duty gives us something to aspire to but also makes personal interests seem trivial. The moral law— and, notably, any person whose integrity and honesty make them an example of the moral law—evokes these feelings in us regardless of whether or not we like it, just as the moral law demands we act from duty whether or not we like it. Kant views this as a familiar dynamic that puts respect in sharp contrast with other feelings we may have. Much of the time, our actions stem from either inclination or fear. We may help a friend move just because we like the company, and many dealers provide transparent pricing because it is good for business or because they fear getting in trouble if exposed. If, however, we put all such inclinations aside and instead do our duty simply because it is our duty, we shall find ourselves animated by the respect we have for the moral law.

Even though Kant's account of duty has so far aligned with much of what commonsense morality tells us, we may also find significant divergences. These will become clear if we explore how Kant contrasts moral duty with other forms of obligation.

While Kant explains duty in terms of how the moral law should shape our motives and actions, we sometimes talk about duty more loosely. Some might say, for instance, that we have a duty to pay taxes or drive on the right side of the road because the government tells us to do so. Although Kant would not recommend that we fail to pay our tax bills or adopt driving on the left side of the road, he would also not grant that the government has the same authority over us as the moral law. The moral law is drawn from our capacity for pure reason, a capacity that doesn't change depending on where or when we live. However, the duties or rules imposed by the government are a product of numerous empirical factors, including where we reside and what legislation has most recently passed. So when we do our moral duty, our motives and actions emanate from an unchanging source of guidance, a feature that distinguishes our moral obligations from all others.

Kant also emphasizes that our willingness to do our moral duty must be uncoerced in a way that has no equivalent in the legal realm. Granted, we can avoid driving on the right side of the road by moving to England, but if we stay in the United States, then agents of the state can, by fines or threats of jail, coerce us to drive on the right side of the road. Note that in a legal context, mere compliance is what matters. Moral duty, by contrast, centers on an inner comportment that cannot be coaxed through force or threats. The moral law elicits a feeling of respect, but our acceptance of the moral law's authority—how we react to those feelings of respect—is a free decision.

Finally, Kant stresses that while some forms of obligation can be outsourced to another person, moral duty cannot. For instance, if we have student loans, what matters to the loan holders is that the debt gets paid in a legally sound way, not that we personally pay it. Moral duty, however, functions differently. When Kant says that duty is our "highest practical function" (Ak. 396), he is saying that doing our duty is a task or vocation each of us must accept. Someone else might be able to take care of our student debt for us, but no one can take over the work we need to do to meet our own moral obligation.

Kant also introduces an important distinction between "perfect" and "imperfect" duties. He characterizes perfect duties as those that are "strict" or "narrow" (Ak. 424). Among these are the duty not to kill ourselves when life proves onerous and the duty not to make promises we cannot keep. He reasons that these duties make exacting demands on us. In no situation are we permitted to choose suicide from a desire for happiness or an aversion to pain, and in no situation can we make a promise we know we cannot keep. Some readers, although not Kant himself, describe these duties as "negative" because they concern acts to refrain from doing. No direct action is needed to avoid taking our own life or making unfulfillable promises.

Imperfect duties include the duty to perfect our talents and help others. These duties work differently from those described previously. These duties are "broad" insofar as they can be fulfilled in a variety of ways. We can cultivate our talents as a cook, community organizer, or teacher. We can help others by signing up for a mutual aid organization or being a companion at an event, even if attending is not our cup of tea. We may also engage in improving ourselves or helping others, whether doing so through many types of activities or focusing only on a few. For that reason, some readers, although not Kant, describe imperfect duties as "positive." To fulfill an imperfect duty, we need to take action toward a particular goal, thereby uniquely stamping this duty with our personal agency. A false promise can be avoided in only one way, but others can be helped in many ways.

Another key difference between imperfect and perfect duties is that the latter never permits "exception in the interest of incli-nation" (Ak. 421, 12n). No matter how intensely or infrequently a person may want to make an unfulfillable promise, doing so is strictly forbidden. In saying, by contrast, that imperfect duties admit exceptions "in the interest of inclination," Kant seems to be suggesting that we need not always actively facilitate our own self-perfection or the well-being of others. While a maxim that advocated even occasional promise-breaking on the grounds of self-interest cannot be universalized, all that Kant rules out in the case of an imperfect duty is a maxim of *never* cultivating our personal talents or *never* tending to the interests of other human beings. Our imperfect duties thus consist in promoting our tal-ents as well as the needs and goals of others. As a result, we can fulfill our imperfect duties even while sometimes we try to satisfy our own interests.

In sum, Kant's account of duty is roughly, though not exactly, in line with our everyday beliefs. We commonly recognize that some duties take priority over others. And while we agree that helping other people is an important goal, we also generally believe it should not be all-consuming or fully interfere with enjoying life. Kant's distinction between imperfect and perfect duties aligns with these intuitions, as the flexibility of fulfilling imperfect duties provides a latitude absent in the case of perfect duties.

Importantly, however, we should not understand Kant's recognizing exceptions to imperfect duties as implying that we can treat imperfect duties like a checklist we occasionally complete to then quickly resume achieving our own happiness. If we are acting from duty, doing so will be at odds with our treating self-perfection or other people's interests as simply a burden to be managed. Similarly, if we attend to our natural talents and serve others, then we will not think of these imperfect duties as "morality lite," less ethically significant than perfect duties. Granted, engaging in self-perfection may be pursued flexibly, but its overarching goal is morally necessary. When, how, and to what extent we discharge an imperfect duty is an open question. Yet that openness should stand alongside a recognition that imperfect and perfect duties alike are only different sides of the same coin, namely, respect for the moral law.

We conclude with two final points regarding something important but unsaid in Kant's account of duty. First, we have no duty to tend to our own happiness. As Kant notes, every human being seeks happiness with "the strongest and deepest inclination" (Ak. 399). Thus Kant sees no need to incorporate concern for our own happiness into his account of duty. Securing one's own happiness could at most count only indirectly as a duty in those circumstances in which "unsatisfied wants" become a "temptation to transgress" against the moral law (Ak. 399).

Second, at least one feature of Kant's discussion of perfect duties remains unsettled: Does Kant want us to generalize the particular examples he gives of perfect duties? For instance, we have a perfect duty not to kill ourselves to avoid physical suffering, but does this principle imply a perfect duty against suicide in all circumstances and for all possible reasons? Similarly, lying to increase our material welfare is a violation of a perfect duty, but suppose the lie stems from a concern to protect others from harm. The answers here are not clear.

On the one hand, Kant's different examples carefully note the circumstances of an action and the reasons behind it. In the example concerning lying, Kant examines not just the action of lying but a maxim or personal principle that advocates lying for the sake of private advantage whenever we can get away with it. This approach suggests that Kant seeks to limit his account of what qualifies as a clear violation of this perfect duty of truth-telling. On the other hand, given Kant's stated interest in a universal moral law that does not make exceptions, would he permit other manifestations of suicide or lying? Again, how Kant intends to address this issue is unclear, but we, too, are torn about whether suicide is always wrong or whether only suicide committed for certain reasons in certain contexts is always wrong. By not providing these answers, Kant leaves us with a challenging puzzle to solve.

4

IMPERATIVES
Tamar Schapiro

The main passages relevant to Imperatives in the *Ground-work* can be found in the following sections: Ak. 413–421.

By the end of the first section of the *Groundwork*, Kant begins to move us beyond commonsense ideas about morally good people and actions toward a more rigorous, philosophical understanding of those ideas. Kant's central aim up to this point has been to remind us of the ways in which moral evaluation is different from other kinds of evaluation and to guide us to inquire further into what this special form of evaluation involves. He does this by asking us to focus on actions that we find morally admirable— those that we take to have "real moral worth" (Ak. 399). In his examples, he tries to bring out something he thinks we already implicitly know, namely, that the actions we regard as having moral worth are all done from a distinct motive. What is this motive? The main function of the examples in the first section is to show us that there is a difference between doing what we happen to want to do and doing what we recognize we ought to do. We can act "from inclination" or "from duty" (Ak. 399). It is only this latter form of motivation, Kant claims, that we take to have distinctively moral value.

In the first part of the second section, Kant continues the same line of inquiry. Can we specify the moral motive even more precisely? It is at this point that he introduces the distinction between a "hypothetical" and a "categorical" imperative (Ak. 414). That distinction is the focus of this essay. I think most readers find it quite a bit easier to understand the concept of a hypothetical imperative than to understand the concept of a categorical imperative. Since the concept of a categorical imperative is central to everything Kant says later in the *Groundwork*, it is important to try to specify it as clearly as we can. I will begin by explaining why Kant feels it necessary to introduce the notion of an imperative shortly after the end of the first section of the *Groundwork*. Next, I will explain how the concept of a hypothetical imperative should be understood. Finally, I will show why it can be difficult to understand the contrasting notion of a categorical imperative, and I will offer a way of resolving that difficulty. My main conclusion is that the concept of a categorical imperative is distinguished not by its grammatical form but by the unique role it is supposed to play in our deliberation.

1. What is Kant's aim in the section on imperatives?

Why does Kant introduce the notion of an imperative at the beginning of the second section? How does this relate to what he has already established in the first section? In the first section, the important distinction was between acting from inclination and acting from duty. But Kant is now aware that the idea of acting from duty can be understood in two different ways. Notice that there is something dutiful about taking the means to your end, even if your end is something you genuinely want. Suppose you are fascinated with Chinese culture, but you did not grow up in that culture. You want to visit China and have an immersive experience, one in which you genuinely learn from those who live there. To do this, you will need to learn Mandarin. Recognizing how difficult it is to learn that language, you might decide not to go further. You might decide you are not really willing to do what it takes to have the immersive experience you want. In that case, although having that experience is the object of your inclination, you decide not to take the further step of making it the object of your will. You stop short of making it your "end." To make it your end would be to commit to bringing it about that you have the immersive experience you want. And that would involve taking responsibility for doing what is necessary to achieve that goal.

Alternatively, suppose you do make it your end to have that immersive experience. You thereby commit yourself to learning Mandarin. You enroll in an intensive language class, which involves a lot of work. You might not feel like doing your language homework on any given day. But you still recognize that you ought to do it, and much of the time, you will choose to do it, even though you do not happen to want to do it at that moment. What this example illustrates is that taking the necessary means to our ends can sometimes be a chore, even when the ends are ends that we genuinely want. Doing your language homework can be a "duty," in something like the sense Kant identified in the first section of the *Groundwork*. It can be something you do because you recognize you ought to do it, regardless of whether you happen to want to do it.

Kant's aim in the section on imperatives is to distinguish this kind of dutiful motivation from the kind of dutiful motivation that has moral worth. All dutiful motivation, as he sees it, is guided by an "imperative" (Ak. 413). An imperative is a command we address to ourselves, of the form "I ought to A . . ." where A refers to an action. When we command ourselves in this way, we recognize the possibility that we might not happen to feel like doing what we ought to do. So the more explicit form of an imperative is "I ought to A, regardless of whether I happen to feel like A'ing . . ." Whereas all dutiful motivation is guided by some imperative or other, Kant's aim is to show us what is distinctive of moral motivation, by showing us that moral motivation is guided by a distinctive type of imperative.

2. What is a hypothetical imperative?

To show what makes moral motivation distinctive, he first tries to explain what the moral motive is not. What it is not is action on a type of imperative that commands "hypothetically" (Ak. 414). Whereas all imperatives "[represent] a possible action as good and hence as necessary" for a person whose actions can be determined "by reason," it is distinctive of a hypothetical imperative that it represents a possible action as good and necessary "merely as a means to something else." That "something else" is something that the person has adopted as her end. In other words, a hypothetical imperative is a guiding thought of the form "I ought to A, regardless of whether I happen to feel like A'ing, because A'ing is necessary to achieve my end E." In the example above, you are guided by a hypothetical imperative that tells you, "I ought to do my Mandarin homework right now, regardless of whether or not I happen to feel like doing so, because doing so is necessary to achieve my end of having an immersive experience in China."

Notice that a hypothetical imperative not only specifies your end but also takes that end to be *given*. I mean that questions about the goodness of E do not have any bearing on the "ought" of a hypothetical imperative. Kant writes:

> Here there is no question at all whether the end is reasonable and good, but there is only a question as to what must be done to attain it. The prescriptions needed by a doctor in order to make his patient thoroughly healthy and by a poisoner in order to make sure of killing his victim are of equal value so far as each serves to bring about its purpose perfectly. (Ak. 415)

It is characteristic of a hypothetical imperative that it addresses you as a technician, in a broad sense of that word. It addresses you as someone who is concerned solely with your own efficacy in achieving an end that you have already decided to achieve. It does not address you as someone who is reflecting on whether you ought to adopt that end in the first place. For this reason, Kant says that a hypothetical imperative commands you, subject to a "condition" (Ak. 416, 420). The condition is that you have already adopted E as your end.[1]

3. What is a categorical imperative?

Now that we understand the concept of a hypothetical imperative, we can ask what a categorical imperative is. How, exactly, does a categorical imperative differ from a hypothetical imperative?

---

1. Kant goes on to distinguish two main types of hypothetical imperatives, corresponding to what are sometimes called the "instrumental" and "prudential" forms of rationality (Ak. 415–416). That distinction is not relevant here, because our focus is on the relation between the general concept of a hypothetical imperative and that of a categorical imperative.

Kant describes this difference in terms that are a bit obscure. He writes:

> Now all imperatives command either hypothetically or categorically. The former represent the practical necessity of a possible action as a means for attaining something else that one wants (or may possibly want). The categorical imperative would be one which represented an action as objectively necessary in itself, without reference to another end. (Ak. 414)

And he continues:

> Now if the action would be good merely as a means *to something else*, so is the imperative *hypothetical*. But if the action is represented as good in itself, and hence as necessary . . . then the imperative is categorical. (Ak. 414, emphasis mine)

A bit further on, he adds:

> [A categorical imperative] is not concerned with the matter of the action and its intended result, but rather with the form of the action and the principle from which it follows. . . . (Ak. 416)

Most readers find it easier to understand the concept of a hypothetical imperative than that of a categorical imperative. Because we have a reasonably clear idea of what it is for an action to be a means to an end, it is not very hard to grasp the concept of valuing an action as a means to an end. But what does it mean to represent an action as "necessary in itself, without reference to another end," or as good in virtue of its "form" rather than its "matter"? And how could it make sense to value an action, so conceived?

The only example Kant gives to illustrate the distinction is this: "You should not make a false promise" commands categorically, as long as it does not tacitly include the further thought, ". . . lest you ruin your credit when the falsity comes to light" (Ak. 419). This imperative, taken as a categorical command, simply says that you should not make a false promise. It says that "an action of this kind must be regarded as bad in itself" (Ak. 419). Now, if we look solely at this example, we might infer that it is possible to construct a categorical imperative by taking any hypothetical imperative and abstracting from the end E. Consider the hypothetical imperative that guides the self-interested shopkeeper in the first section. "I ought not treat this inexperienced customer unfairly, lest, if it became known, I would destroy my reputation." Presumably, if he were acting in a morally worthy way, he would act on the imperative, "I ought not treat this inexperienced customer unfairly." In a similar fashion, we can consider examples that have nothing to do with self-interested ends. When it comes to keeping promises, you should not be guided by an imperative that says, "I ought to keep my promise to her, because doing so would make her happy," but rather one that says, "I ought to keep my promise to her." When it comes to telling the truth, you should not be guided by an imperative that says, "I ought to tell him the truth, because doing so would make him happy," but rather, "I ought to tell him the truth."

Although this makes a kind of intuitive sense, it becomes odd when we consider the examples of hypothetical imperatives that Kant actually has in mind in this section. Take the doctor's imperative, "I ought to treat this patient with this medication, because doing so will cure her disease." Is Kant's thought that the doctor who acts in a morally worthy way acts instead on the imperative, "I ought to treat this patient with this medication," regardless of whether doing so will cure the patient's disease and regardless of whether or not it is the doctor's end to cure the patient's disease? That would be absurd. Consider the poisoner's maxim, "I ought to administer this poison to this person, because doing so will kill him." Does the poisoner become more worthy of esteem by instead acting on "I ought to administer this poison to this person," regardless of whether doing so will kill him and regardless of whether the poisoner has made it his end to kill that person? Surely not. So what is Kant trying to say?

I suggest that a better interpretation starts from the idea that a categorical imperative is distinguished by the unique role it plays in deliberation. Recall that a hypothetical imperative guides you on the condition that your end is already *given*, in the sense that you have already made it the object of your will. I interpreted that to mean that hypothetical imperatives address us as technicians. They address us as people who are already committed to bringing about some end E, and who are solely concerned with being efficacious. They do not address us as people trying to decide whether and why we should make E our end. A categorical imperative, by contrast, addresses us as reflective agents who think not only about the efficacy of our actions but also about their goodness in some other sense. What is that other sense?

Suppose you are already committed to following the Ten Commandments. If that is the case, you will be concerned not only with your efficacy but also with whether you are acting in ways that conform to the Ten Commandments. You will not administer the poison, regardless of any ends you might have set, because doing so violates the sixth commandment, "Thou shalt not kill." But I think Kant's view is that even this way of reflecting on the goodness of your action would still be conditional. The condition is that you have already made it your end to follow the Ten Commandments. Or, put a bit differently, the condition is that you are already committed to being a conscientious servant of God, which means following His will, as expressed in the Ten Commandments.

Kant holds that moral motivation is distinctive, because it is unconditional in an even stronger sense. The moral imperative addresses us as agents who are not yet bound by *any* condition. This means we have not yet made any commitment, either to bring about some end, to follow some set of rules, or to obey the will of some ruler. A categorical imperative would be a command that addresses us as people who are concerned with the goodness of our actions but are not yet committed to any particular standard of good action. It would be an imperative that addresses us as free, in the sense that we have not yet signed on to any substantive conception of what acting well consists in.

This is the concept of a categorical imperative that Kant is appealing to when he makes his key argumentative move:

> If I think of a hypothetical imperative in general, I do not know beforehand what it will contain until its condition is given. But if I think of a categorical imperative, I know immediately what it contains. For since, besides the law, the imperative contains only the necessity that the maxim should accord with this law, while the law includes no conditions to restrict it, there remains nothing but the universality of a law as such with which the maxim of the action should conform. This conformity alone is properly what is represented as necessary by the imperative. (Ak. 420–421)

Kant claims that we can derive the content of the categorical imperative from nothing more than the bare concept of a categorical imperative. The concept of a categorical imperative is not that of a rule with a certain grammatical form, namely "Do A!" Any rule of that form would have to derive the content of A from some prior and independent source. Rather, the concept of a categorical imperative is that of something that plays a certain role in deliberation. That role is to command a person who is both free and trying to act well. What is the content of an imperative that could be addressed to you as such a person? Assume you are not already committed to any ends, set of rules, or ultimate source of authority, like God or a sacred text. But assume you also care about living your life in a way that does not amount to simply giving in to your inclinations, moment to moment. You care about living your life according to some standard of goodness, one that could, in principle, require you to do what you ought to do, rather than what you happen to want to do. What rule could you adopt from that standpoint?

Kant's answer is that when you are in that standpoint, you are already tacitly committed to the idea that to act well is to act on some imperative or other. This commitment alone, he believes, provides the key to answering the question. Any imperative, regardless of its content, has a certain form. Its form is that of "universal law."

> Hence there is only one categorical imperative and it is this: Act only according to that maxim whereby you can at the same time will that it should become a universal law. (Ak. 421)

The idea is something like this: given that you are already committed to acting well, you are already committed to acting on some guiding thought of the form "I ought to A, regardless of whether I happen to want to A." Now, your way of governing yourself might initially be something you only value conditionally. The hired assassin overcomes her laziness, gets out of bed, and does her poisoning duty in order to get her reward. She values her action for its efficacy in getting her the reward she wants. But if she were to reflect on why she values the end of assassinating people, why she accepts the rules that structure her profession, or why she follows the wills of those who hire her, she would have to ask deeper questions about what this way of governing herself consists in, and about what she is upholding when she is participating in this way of life. Kant thinks that ultimately she would have to ask herself whether what she is doing is something she can do in a principled way, whether it is something she can "will" as "a universal law." It is this sort of reflection that Kant takes to be distinctive of moral motivation.

Similarly, we can imagine a Christian who overcomes her laziness, gets out of bed, and does her charity service in order to get her neighbors' approval. She values her action for its efficacy in maintaining the public reputation that she wants. But if she were to reflect on why she values the end of being thought of as a charitable person, why she accepts the rules that structure her religious practice, or why she follows the wills of those who have authority in her church, she would have to ask deeper questions about what this way of governing herself consists in, and about what she is upholding when she is participating in this way of life. Kant thinks that ultimately she would have to ask herself whether what she is doing is something she can do in a principled way, whether it is something she can "will" as a "universal law." Insofar as she engages in this sort of reflection, she is asking whether she can find a genuinely moral motive for endorsing the kind of life that she has been leading.

We do not yet really understand what Kant means by "universal law" or how it is that some actions can, and others cannot, be willed as such. But the outline of Kant's argument is now at least intelligible. The concept of a categorical imperative is not that of a truncated hypothetical imperative. It is not the concept of a rule that takes the grammatical form, "Do A!" Rather, it is the concept of a command that plays a unique role in deliberation.

Its function is to guide you as a free person who cares about acting well. If there is such a standard, it is one that you could accept unconditionally, as someone who is not yet committed to any prior and independent standard of action, whether that takes the form of a given end, a given set of rules, or a given authoritative ruler. Kant believes such a standard does exist, because in asking for it, you are already committed to acting in a certain way. You are already committed to governing yourself, and according to Kant, that means you are already committed to acting only on universal laws. Nevertheless, it remains to be seen whether a command that tells you nothing more than to act only on universal laws can actually serve as a helpful guide in the course of living your life.

5

THE FORMULA OF UNIVERSAL LAW

Kyla Ebels-Duggan

The main passages relevant to the Formula of Universal Law in the *Groundwork* can be found in the following sections: Ak. 420–424; related passages can be found at Ak. 402–403 and 436–437.

In the first section of the *Groundwork for the Metaphysics of Morals*, Kant begins with the idea of a good will and argues to an initial statement of the principle on which he claims a good-willed, or virtuous, person would act: "I should never act except in such a way that I can also will that my maxim should become a universal law" (Ak. 402). In *Groundwork II*, he begins again with a different idea, the concept of an *imperative*, that is, a directive or command. He asks what could make a purported imperative genuine: Under what conditions are we really obligated to follow a command (Ak. 413, 417)?

The answer, Kant argues, depends on what sort of imperative it is. A *hypothetical imperative* requires you to do something on the condition that you aim to accomplish something else. It takes for granted some goal or purpose and tells you what you must do to achieve it. For example, *if you aim to get to class on time, leave by 9:00 a.m.* But the fundamental moral principle could not be like this. It cannot depend on what you want or on which aims you happen to have. If there is a moral principle, it must be a different kind of imperative—a *categorical imperative*, a requirement without any conditions or assumptions attached. It would have to be an unconditional requirement.

It is far from obvious how there could be any such unconditional requirement or, as Kant puts it, how a categorical imperative is possible (Ak. 417). Kant won't complete his answer to this question until the third and final section, but in *Groundwork II* he takes the first essential step. To determine whether there could be a categorical imperative, he thinks we must first ask: If there were a categorical imperative, what would it be? That is to say, what content *could* a categorical imperative have? This is the question that he takes up in the second section.

Kant has a bold strategy for addressing this question. He says he will "inquire whether perhaps the mere concept of a categorical imperative may not also supply us with the formula containing the proposition that can alone be a categorical imperative" (Ak. 420). That is, beginning with nothing but the idea of an unconditional requirement, he will try to arrive at a conclusion about what The Categorical Imperative is or—as he puts it—what it contains (Ak. 420). He aims to derive the *content* of The Categorical Imperative from the *concept* of a categorical imperative.

Kant seems to think that this ambitious plan succeeds rather easily. Shortly after announcing it, he says:

> But if I think of a categorical imperative, I know immediately what it contains. For since, besides the law, the imperative contains only the necessity that the maxim should

accord with this law, while the law contains no condition to restrict it, there remains nothing but the universality of a law as such with which the maxim of action should conform. This conformity alone is properly what is represented as necessary by the imperative.

Hence there is only one categorical imperative and it is this: Act only according to that maxim whereby you can at the same time will that it should become a universal law. (Ak. 420–421)

Maybe Kant really does know this "immediately," but his readers usually need to take things a bit more slowly. Here's the basic outline of his reasoning: A categorical imperative would be an unconditional requirement. It would be a directive you have to follow whether you want to or not and no matter what else you aim to do. In this way, it would be like a law. That's the *concept* of a categorical imperative. Since the concept is all that we have, we can't assume anything further about the content of this law— exactly what it says or what it tells us to do. All that we can say is that a categorical imperative would direct us to *act on a law*. That is, whatever your principle—what Kant calls your maxim— of action is, it has to be fit to be a law; it has to be a principle that could be a law.[1] And so Kant concludes his terse argument with his (somewhat cumbersome) statement of the Formula of Universal Law: "Act only according to that maxim whereby you can at the same time will that it should become a universal law" (Ak. 421). With that, he brings the inquiry about whether the concept

---

1. Christine M. Korsgaard, *The Sources of Normativity* (Cambridge: Cambridge University Press, 1996), 90–100. Cf. Christine M. Korsgaard, *Fellow Creatures: Our Obligations to the Other Animals* (Oxford: Oxford University Press, 2018), 118–22.

of a categorical imperative will yield its formula to a quick and successful end.

But the reader is likely left with many questions about how to understand this formula and what sort of use it could be. Important among these: What, exactly, does it mean to say that I *can will* the principle on which I act as a universal law? Can we make sense of this idea in a way that includes some principles of action while ruling out others? And will the sorting that results plausibly track something of moral significance?

In directing you to consider whether your maxim can be universalized, the Formula of Universal Law suggests a familiar moral question: What if everyone did that? Or how would you like it if someone did that to you? But we need to be careful: the Formula of Universal Law isn't exactly about what you would *like*. Kant makes this explicit in a footnote, where he compares the Golden Rule—do unto others as you *would have them* do unto you—unfavorably to his own moral principle (Ak. 430, 23n). Because it depends on your preferences, a principle like that would be more like a hypothetical imperative. After all, you might want weird or idiosyncratic things, or you might not care if people treat you in some ways that they really shouldn't. Nor can the principle direct you to ask what you *should* will as a universal law. Answering that question would require some account of what makes some principles ones that you have to follow no matter what else you want or aim at. But that's exactly the question that Kant intends his derivation of the content of The Categorical Imperative from the concept of a categorical imperative to answer. If we need an account of which principles we should will in order to interpret the conclusion of this derivation, then the derivation will have done nothing to advance our understanding.

Rather than *would* or *should* or *may*, Kant really does mean *can* here. He is talking about what it is *possible* to will. But the possibility that the Formula of Universal Law directs us to assess is not just that of willing a particular maxim. People do choose to violate moral requirements with some regularity, so it is obviously possible to do so. Instead, the possibility on which Kant focuses is that of willing a maxim as your own principle of action and *at the same time* willing that maxim as a universal law. He believes that this is not possible for just any principle. Some principles, he holds, contradict their own universalization.

Compare believing a contradiction—say, believing that we have potatoes in the pantry and, at the same time, believing that we do not have potatoes in the pantry. Either of these beliefs might be reasonable on its own, but they cannot form a rational set since they cannot both be true at the same time. Further, since believing something is regarding it as true, there is a clear sense in which it is not even *possible* to hold these two beliefs at the same time, at least not in a clear-eyed way. It's not just that you shouldn't do that or wouldn't *like* to (maybe sometimes you *would* like to). Holding contradictory beliefs is unintelligible and so can't really count as holding the beliefs at all.

Kant thinks there is a similar sense in which some practical principles cannot be willed as your own maxim of action and, at the same time, be willed as a universal law: doing so would generate some sort of contradiction. But how should we understand this contradiction? Kant doesn't explain that directly but instead gives four examples of maxims that he thinks contradict their own universalization. We can try to extract from these examples the sense of contradiction he has in mind.

To begin, let's focus on the second of these examples, the lying promise, which is usually thought to provide the most straightforward illustration of Kant's approach. In this example, a man needs money. To get it, he asks for a loan and promises to pay it back, though he doesn't intend to actually do so. Kant says that if this maxim were universalized, it would contradict itself, observing that, in that case, everyone would laugh at assurances of repayment as vain pretense (Ak. 422).

Some commentators have tried to understand the contradiction Kant finds here as just like the contradiction between beliefs that we just considered. That sort of view has proven to be difficult to work out because *willing* something is importantly different from *believing* it. To will something is not to regard it as true but to undertake to accomplish it. It is one thing to think we have potatoes in the pantry and quite another to decide to acquire some potatoes. So, if principles of action are to contradict each other, it can't be because they can't be believed together. It has to be because they can't be willed or acted on together: they commit you to incompatible aims. This is a distinctively practical sort of contradiction.[2]

To see how this goes in the case of the lying promise, we need first to formulate the relevant maxim, that is, what the man in the example is proposing to do. This maxim has to state both the intended act and the aim with which it is undertaken, what the agent is trying to accomplish. In this case, the maxim is *I will make a lying promise in order to access some money.* Next, we need to universalize the maxim. How, exactly, we should think about the universal correlate of a given principle is not obvious, but as a first attempt, let's try this: willing a universalized maxim means willing a situation in which everyone with an aim like yours tries to accomplish it in the same way that you propose to. Here, *I will that anyone who needs some money makes a lying promise.* Call the situation that is willed here the World of the Universalized Maxim.

---

2. Here and below, I draw on Christine Korsgaard, "Kant's Formula of Universal Law," chap. 3, in *Creating the Kingdom of Ends* (Cambridge: Cambridge University Press, 1996). Cf. John Rawls, *Lectures on the History of Moral Philosophy* (Cambridge, MA: Harvard University Press, 2000), 162–80.

Now to see whether we have a practical contradiction, we ask: In the World of the Universalized Maxim, would the proposed action effectively accomplish the relevant end? Here, *If everyone who needs money makes a lying promise to get it, will lying promises be an effective means of securing funds?* Kant thinks the answer is clearly negative: if lying promises were the universal method for accessing money, no one would believe them. So, if the person in Kant's example were to will his maxim and at the same time will the World of the Universalized Maxim, he would be involved in a practical contradiction. In willing the maxim, he wills the aim it specifies: getting the money. But in willing the World of the Universalized Maxim, he would undermine this same aim. Like contradictory beliefs, these two attitudes cannot be held together, at least not in a clear-eyed way.

So interpreted, the Formula of Universal Law plausibly flags maxims on which it would be impermissible to act; it tells you *that* acting on some maxim would be wrong. But it also does something further. It specifies what makes some maxims impermissible; it tells you *how* acting on some maxims would be wrong. The Formula of Universal Law is not like a mysterious guru or an oracle that simply issues directives about what you may and may not do. Instead, it provides a way of thinking about your actions that transparently displays the feature on account of which it sorts them into the permissible and the impermissible.

Kant identifies the problem with an impermissible maxim as "making an exception to the law for yourself" (Ak. 424). This is a recognizably moral idea associated with the moral ideal of *equality*. If everyone has equal standing, then the same rules should govern us all.[3] On the interpretation above, you violate this ideal

---

3. Cf. Karen Stohr, "The Categorical Imperative: Equality," chap. 5, in *Choosing Freedom* (New York: Oxford University Press, 2022).

when the success of your action depends on others acting differently. In willing your maxim, you allow yourself to act in a way that not everyone could act. That might indeed seem intuitively morally objectionable, and it's plausibly the feature of an action the familiar moral question "What if everyone did that?" is supposed to highlight.

But this way of thinking about what makes a maxim wrong is vulnerable to some important counterexamples. In some cases, it seems not to rule out enough; it produces false positives, making some impermissible maxims look permissible. For example, suppose people are almost always able to repay their loans and make false promises only in the very rare instances where they can't. Because there would then be many sincere promises of repayment, people wouldn't necessarily laugh at a lying promise, and it could be an effective means of securing a loan. The method the agent proposes to undertake would still work in the World of the Universalized Maxim. So, on the interpretation we're considering, the Formula of Universal Law would say that making a lying promise is permissible in this situation. But it doesn't seem like the permissibility of false promises should depend, in this way, on how frequently people make them.

Additionally, you might think it's not true that every case in which your action works only because others act differently involves you in treating others as if they are not your moral equals. This raises a different worry: on the interpretation above, the formula appears to rule out too much, making permissible maxims look impermissible and producing false negatives. Consider the maxim: *I will play tennis early on Sunday mornings to avoid crowds.*[4] This seems like an unobjectionable proposal, yet

4. The example is taken from Barbara Herman, "Moral Deliberation and the Derivation of Duties," chap. 7 in *The Practice of Moral Judgment* (Cambridge, MA: Harvard University Press (1993), 138–39.

the plan will manifestly fail if everyone who aims to play tennis in the absence of crowds adopts it.

This suggests that we should rethink our conception of universalization and revise the question we're supposed to ask about our maxims to capture the ideal of moral equality better. One possibility is to ask, not what would happen if everyone *did* act on your maxim, but what would happen if everyone *regarded it as permissible* to do so? Could you succeed in accomplishing your end if you announced publicly, in advance of acting, that it is permissible for anyone to act in this way? On that way of approaching things, the World of the Universalized Maxim is one in which anyone may act on your maxim if they choose to, and everyone knows this, but people won't necessarily choose to. If you cannot accomplish your aim by acting on the maxim in those circumstances, then your maxim contradicts its universalization and is shown to be impermissible.

Understanding the test this way seems to get the cases discussed above right. The lying promise will fail. You cannot secure a loan by promising to pay it back if it is a public fact that it is permissible to make such a promise insincerely. Imagine saying: "It's permissible to make a lying promise, and if you loan me money, I promise I will pay it back." Even if false promises aren't all that common, people will laugh at this, and it won't be an effective way of getting the money you need. So it looks like this way of thinking of the formula eliminates the false positive. And the revised approach also yields the intuitively correct answer in the tennis case. It *is* possible to avoid crowds by hitting the tennis courts early on Sunday mornings, even if everyone knows this is a permissible way of acting. In fact, it is not just possible but actual: most people regard playing tennis on Sunday mornings as permissible, yet this method of crowd-avoidance continues to work.

Perhaps most importantly, this way of thinking of the test provides a better interpretation of the problem of making an exception for yourself and the underlying ideal of moral equality. The moral problem is not that your action works only because others don't act that way. Cases of permissible coordination, like the tennis example, show that can be perfectly fine: there's no suggestion that those who spend their Sunday mornings in some other way are not your moral equals. Rather, you make an objectionable exception for yourself when the success of your action depends on others regarding it as impermissible for them to act as you do. Here, you require that others accept that rules that don't bind you nevertheless apply to them and that is an affront to moral equality.

So far, we've been focusing on the lying promise example, but Kant also gives three others. He doesn't choose these cases randomly. Rather, each one represents a category of duties. Kant believes that duties may be owed to others or to ourselves and that they may be—in a way I will explain below—either perfect or imperfect. These two divisions cut across each other to generate the four categories:

	Duties to Others	**Duties to Yourself**
Perfect	The duty to keep promises	The duty not to commit suicide
Imperfect	The duty of beneficence	The duty to develop your talents

Perfect duties are specific acts or omissions, usually owed to a particular person. The duty not to make a lying promise is perfect. Kant also calls this sort of duty strict or narrow. Imperfect duties, by contrast, are obligations to adopt some end but don't specify exactly what or how much you must do to pursue it. Imperfect duties direct you to value something, but they allow discretion about how to express or demonstrate your commitment to that value. While violating a perfect duty usually wrongs someone in particular—e.g., the promisee in the case of the lying promise—violating an imperfect duty often does not. Kant says that perfect and imperfect duties contradict their universalization in different ways. Maxims that violate perfect duties are, he says, impossible to *think* along with their universalization. Those that violate imperfect duties can be thought but are impossible to *will* along with their universalization (Ak. 424).

So far, I've just been focusing on the first sort of problem, what is often called a contradiction in conception.[5] As we've seen, that contradiction arises when willing the universalization of the maxim undermines the aim stated in the maxim. But maxims that violate imperfect duties don't state an aim at all. Instead, they announce a refusal to adopt one. Kant offers two examples:

1. A maxim of non-development of talents: *I will neglect my natural gifts.*

2. A maxim of non-beneficence: *I will not offer assistance to others.*

We need some account of what Kant means when he says these maxims cannot be willed as universal laws. Here's a way to understand what he is up to: The employment of human skills and talents—your own or others—is the *only* way to accomplish an end. Whatever you aim to do, either you can do it yourself, and thus need your own talents, or you can do it with the help of others and thus need their assistance. If everyone failed to develop their talents or everyone failed to offer help, then there would

---

5. Cf. Korsgaard, "Kant's Formula," 78.

be no resources to do anything and all of your ends would be undermined. So, if you have any aims or purposes at all, you cannot at the same time will the universalization of either of these two maxims.

While not exactly like the contradiction in conception that arises in the case of maxims violating perfect duties, this contradiction highlights a similar moral problem of making an unwarranted exception for yourself and so refusing to acknowledge the moral equality of others. Here the problem is like that of the free rider: you depend on, or make use of, a collective good for achieving your ends but do not do your part to contribute to the collective good. The collective good at issue here is the pool of human talents and powers. To contribute fairly to this resource, you must both do something to develop your own abilities and be willing to make these abilities available to others to some extent.

We have seen how Kant derives the Formula of Universal Law from the mere concept, the very idea, of a categorical imperative. We have seen what he means by saying that some maxims cannot be willed together with their universalization on pain of generating a contradiction. We have seen how this contradiction is distinctively practical and how it appears in similar, yet distinct, guises in violations of perfect and imperfect duties, respectively.

If these arguments succeed, the formula is not empty, as some critics of Kant have suggested: some maxims fail to meet the standard it sets while others succeed in doing so. Moreover, we have interpreted the test in a way that makes sense of regarding this failure as morally significant. But there are two important things the Formula of Universal Law doesn't accomplish. First, it does not replace or eliminate the need for moral judgment. Even if the universalization test works as advertised, you must exercise judgment in formulating the relevant maxim. There may be several accurate descriptions of what you are doing, but only some of these will include the morally significant features of the situation and action. The formula does not tell you which to select. You will also need to exercise judgment in determining what it means for others to have an aim "like yours" and to undertake an action "like yours." Nor will it always be obvious or straightforward whether your actions work in the World of the Universalized Maxim.

Although interpreters, both sympathetic and critical, have sometimes looked to the Formula of Universal Law for an algorithm that would allow us to derive duties from merely descriptive, evaluatively neutral features of the world and action, this imposes a role on the formula that Kant did not intend for it to play.[6] Indeed, it would be quite surprising if any moral theory could substitute for moral judgment. The best moral theories are, instead, those that point us to the right *questions* to ask about actions we are considering. We may assess Kant's Formula of Universal Law in this light. The formula takes a stand on how we should think about the permissibility of our actions. It directs you to ask, "Can I will my maxim as a universal law?" I have explained how this can, in turn, be interpreted as a version of the questions, "Am I making an unwarranted exception for myself?" or "Am I treating others as my moral equals?" We approach these questions by asking a more specific one: "Does my action work only because I am allowing myself to do something that I could not at the same time allow others to do?"

Importantly, this way of thinking about what you are doing is distinct from alternatives. Act utilitarianism tells you to ask whether your action maximizes overall net happiness. Some virtue theorists tell you to ask whether so acting is conducive to your flourishing. The Formula of Universal Law might be

---

6. Cf. Herman, "Moral Deliberation."

getting the important moral question—or at least an important moral question—right, even if it doesn't supply a mechanical test for answering that question. It can function as an aid to moral judgment, without replacing moral judgment, by focusing our attention on this question.

Secondly, the formula is not self-vindicating. We've seen how it can guide our thinking about whether some way of acting would be wrong, and we've seen the account of what makes an action wrong that it supplies. But the formula does not tell us *why* it would be wrong to make an exception for ourselves. If we accept the ideal of moral equality on which Kant's formula draws, then we will see ourselves as having reasons to act as the Formula of Universal Law directs. But Kant makes no attempt in this section of the *Groundwork* to address skepticism about this ideal.

To see what I mean, contrast the situation of the man making the lying promise with a case in which someone points out that you have contradictory beliefs. In that latter case, you wouldn't need any further account of why you have to revise your beliefs in some way. Indeed, it is unclear what such an account could come to. Violations of the hypothetical imperative are a practical version of this same sort of thing: if you recognize that you are willing some end, and failing to will the necessary means to that end, you thereby see a compelling reason to somehow revise what you will.

In both of those cases, there is a contradiction between your *actual* attitudes. These attitudes form an incoherent set and put you at odds with yourself. The lying promise and other violations of the Formula of Universal Law are different. Kant does not claim here that your maxim contradicts itself. The contradiction—the undermining of a purpose that you will— only arises if you will the maxim *along with its universalization*.

That's, of course, exactly what that formula directs you to do or at least think about whether you could do. But the formula itself doesn't explain why you ought to perform that thought experiment or why you should care about its results. To explain that would be to show that the candidate moral law Kant has articulated is genuine and really does have authority. This is the "special and difficult effort" (Ak. 420) of explaining how a categorical imperative is possible, a task Kant takes up in *Groundwork III*.

6

THE FORMULA OF HUMANITY

Japa Pallikkathayil

The main passages relevant to the Formula of Humanity in the *Groundwork* can be found in the following sections: Ak. 396 and Ak. 413–438.

Kant identifies what he calls the categorical imperative as the supreme moral principle. Although Kant claims that there is just one categorical imperative, he formulates it in different ways. This essay focuses on the second formulation of the categorical imperative, the Formula of Humanity. The Formula of Humanity holds: "Act in such a way that you treat humanity, whether in your own person or in the person of another, always at the same time as an end and never simply as a means" (Ak. 429). This essay begins by addressing why Kant takes the categorical imperative to be formulable in these terms. I then explain what it means to treat humanity always as an end and never simply as a means by working through the four examples Kant uses in the *Groundwork* to show how duties are derived from the Formula of Humanity.

Imperatives formulate commands of reason (Ak. 413). A hypothetical imperative commands that one take the means to one's ends. You might, for example, set yourself the end of becoming a doctor. You are then subject to a hypothetical imperative to take the means to this end, for example, going to medical school. In this case, the imperative presents going to medical school as to be done in order to become a doctor. In contrast, a categorical imperative "immediately commands a certain conduct without having as its condition any other purpose to be attained by it" (Ak. 416). A categorical imperative does not command conduct for the sake of bringing about any further end. In this way, a categorical imperative commands unconditionally.

Kant claims that reflection on the concept of a categorical imperative reveals the content such an imperative would have (Ak. 420). Since a categorical imperative commands unconditionally, it has the form of a law. Thus, reflection on the concept of a categorical imperative reveals that such an imperative would require one to act as if following a law. This observation brings Kant to the first formulation of the categorical imperative, the Formula of Universal Law: "Act only according to that maxim whereby you can at the same time will that it should become a universal law" (Ak. 421). A maxim is a combination of an act and an end, for example, "I will go swimming in order to cool off." In this maxim, going swimming is the act and cooling off is the end. The Formula of Universal Law evaluates maxims by assessing whether they could be followed universally. Could everyone in your circumstances act similarly? If not, you would be acting in a way that makes an exception for yourself. This is the basic moral mistake identified by the Formula of Universal Law (Ak. 424).

Notice that the kind of exception for oneself that is the focus of the Formula of Universal Law differs from the kind of exception for oneself that is the focus of the familiar "Golden Rule" to treat others as you want to be treated. What the Golden Rule requires of you depends on what you happen to desire. You do not violate the Golden Rule by, for example, lying to others, as long as you are content with being treated likewise. In contrast, the commands of the Formula of Universal Law do not depend on what you happen to desire. Rather the Formula of Universal Law is concerned with whether your ability to act on a maxim depends in some way on others, at least sometimes, acting differently. If so, then acting on that maxim involves making an exception for yourself even if you would not mind being treated similarly.

Kant builds from the Formula of Universal Law to the Formula of Humanity by reflecting on the nature of action. We act on the basis of ends (Ak. 427). Thus, acting in the way the Formula of Universal Law commands must be done with some end in view. But reflection on the concept of a categorical imperative reveals that this end would differ from ordinary ends like becoming a doctor or cooling off in two important respects. First, since a categorical imperative commands unconditionally, it would need to relate our actions to an unconditional end of all rational beings, that is, beings capable of setting ends for themselves. Second, since a categorical imperative does not command actions for the sake of bringing about some further end, it would need to relate our actions to this unconditional end in a different way. In what follows, I first consider what could serve as an unconditional end for all rational beings. I then consider how our actions could relate to this end without treating it as something to be brought about.

Let us begin by considering what could serve as an unconditional end for all rational beings. The value of such an end could not depend on the idiosyncratic features of particular rational beings, like what they happen to desire. But if an end "is given by reason alone, then it must be equally valid for all rational beings"

(Ak. 427). Are there any ends that we are rationally required to have? Kant claims that something that has absolute worth in itself, that is, value apart from anything it brought about, would be such an end. And he claims that only rational beings themselves have this kind of value. To support this claim, he surveys other potential objects of value and finds that none of them are valuable in themselves (Ak. 428). The objects of our inclinations have only conditional value because they would not be valuable in the absence of those inclinations. Cooling off is valuable only because I want to be cool. Could inclinations themselves be unconditionally valuable? Kant claims that rational beings would prefer to be free from inclinations because they give rise to needs. Although he does not explain this point further, perhaps his thought is that inclinations leave us vulnerable to a certain kind of disappointment when they are not satisfied. Hence inclinations are far from having value in themselves (Ak. 428). Consider next happiness. Although Kant holds that all finite rational beings may be assumed to have their own happiness as an end, earlier in the *Groundwork* Kant argues that happiness has only conditional value (Ak. 396). Happiness is valuable only when it is the happiness of someone with a good, that is, moral, will.

We have seen that neither the objects of our inclinations, the inclinations themselves, nor the happiness to which the satisfaction of inclination contributes have unconditional value. What about beings who exist independently of our actions, like animals? Kant asserts without argument that non-rational beings have value only as means and hence have only conditional value. In contrast, he claims that rational beings have the kind of value we have been looking for: they have unconditional value as ends in themselves. He argues that we can see this because this is how we each necessarily think of our own existence and that others must likewise see themselves this way (Ak. 429).

Why must you view yourself as having unconditional value as a rational being? You must see the ends you pursue as worth pursuing. You may see them as valuable because they satisfy your inclinations or contribute to your happiness. But this cannot be the end of the story, because our inclinations and happiness also have at most conditional value. To bring this chain of conditional values to a close, you must see yourself as having unconditional value, that is, as an end in yourself.[1] In other words, to see the satisfaction of your inclinations and your happiness as mattering, you must see yourself as mattering. Your ends are valuable because they are pursued by someone who is valuable.

So far, we have considered what could serve as an unconditional end for all rational beings, and we have found that rational beings are themselves this end. Let us return to the second issue noted above. Recall that since a categorical imperative does not command actions for the sake of bringing about some further end, it would need to relate our actions to this unconditional end in a different way. Acting to bring something into existence is not the only way of treating something as valuable. We can also recognize something of already existing value as something that constrains our actions. This is how Kant proposes that we relate to the value of rational beings. We are to conceive of this end "only negatively, i.e., as an end which should never be acted against" (Ak. 437). Thus, to say that we must always treat rational beings as ends in themselves is not to say that we should set about bringing more rational beings into existence. Rather, it is to say that we must conduct ourselves with deference to their value, a value that exists independently of our choices.

---

1. Christine M. Korsgaard, "Kant's Formula of Humanity," chap. 4, in *Creating the Kingdom of Ends* (Cambridge: Cambridge University Press, 1996), 116–18.

While the Formula of Universal Law characterizes the form all maxims must have, the Formula of Humanity identifies the end they must all have (Ak. 436). Although Kant's reference to "humanity" in the Formula of Humanity naturally suggests that the categorical imperative is specifically concerned with the treatment of human beings, he often uses the terms humanity and rational nature interchangeably.[2] He is also clear in the above argument that all rational beings must be treated as ends in themselves (Ak. 428, 431). The Formula of Humanity is thus best read as directing us to treat rational beings always as ends in themselves and not simply as means, whether those rational beings are human or not.

We will get a clearer sense of what this means in practice by working through the four examples Kant gives of duties derived from the Formula of Humanity. These four examples highlight two distinctions between duties. The first distinction is between duties to oneself and duties to others. This distinction highlights a noteworthy aspect of Kant's view. For Kant, morality is not solely about our treatment of others. We have duties to ourselves that have the same basis and force as our duties to others.

The second distinction at work in Kant's four examples is between perfect and imperfect duties. Kant describes perfect duties, which he also calls necessary or strict, as permitting "no exception in the interest of inclination" (Ak. 422, 12n). Although this might seem to suggest that imperfect duties admit such exceptions, Kant's examples suggest that imperfect duties differ from perfect duties by virtue of having different objects. Perfect duties are duties to perform or abstain from particular actions. Imperfect duties are duties to pursue certain ends. As we will see, since ends can often be pursued in different ways, we have

---

2. Korsgaard, "Kant's Formula of Humanity," 110.

more flexibility about how to satisfy imperfect duties. This does not mean that imperfect duties admit of exceptions. Rather, this means only that imperfect duties do not generally require specific actions in the way that perfect duties do.

With these distinctions in mind, we may turn to consider Kant's four examples. His first example is of a perfect duty to oneself. Here he envisions a man contemplating suicide:

> [He] will ask himself whether his action can be consistent with the idea of humanity as an end in itself. If he destroys himself in order to escape from a difficult situation, then he is making use of his person merely as a means so as to maintain a tolerable condition till the end of his life. Man, however, is not a thing and hence not something to be used merely as a means; he must in all his actions always be regarded as an end in himself. (Ak. 429)

The argument in this passage focuses on establishing a perfect duty not to kill oneself in order to escape from difficult situations. Kant claims suicide committed for this reason would involve treating oneself merely as a means. How so? Recall that in the example I gave above, going to medical school was a means to becoming a doctor. Here medical school is valued for what it can bring about. In the case of suicide being considered, the man values himself only as a means to maintain a "tolerable condition." In other words, he values himself only for the positive experiences he might come to have. So, if his continued life will not yield such experiences, he regards himself as having no value worth preserving. In this sense, he treats himself merely as a means and not as an end in himself.

What does this argument suggest about suicide for other reasons or other forms of self-harm? Kant seems to draw a general conclusion from the above argument but then immediately qualifies it:

> Therefore, I cannot dispose of man in my own person by mutilating, damaging, or killing him. (A more exact determination of this principle so as to avoid all misunderstanding, e.g., regarding the amputation of limbs in order to save oneself, or the exposure of one's life to danger in order to save it, and so on, must here be omitted; such questions belong to morals proper.) (Ak. 429)

This passage suggests that we cannot easily move from the argument against killing oneself to escape difficult situations to a more general condemnation of suicide and self-harm. Rather, the purposes for which these actions are undertaken matter.

Next, let us consider Kant's second example, which concerns a perfect duty to others not to make false promises. A false promise is one made without intending to fulfill it. When Kant first introduces the example of a false promise to elucidate the Formula of Universal Law, he considers a man in need who finds himself "forced to borrow money. He knows well that he won't be able to repay it, but he sees also that he will not get any loan unless he firmly promises to repay it within a fixed time" (Ak. 422). Here the false promise would be to repay the money, knowing he will not do so.

When Kant evaluates this action with the Formula of Humanity, he argues that the false promisor treats the lender merely as a means to escape financial hardship. To establish this, it is not sufficient to observe that the false promisor uses the lender's actions for his own purposes. We very often do that in unproblematic ways. For example, you might learn from a professor's lecture, dine at a chef's restaurant, or be driven home by a friend. In all these cases, someone's action contributes to your ends. But although these are ways of using the others' actions, they need not involve treating them merely as a means. What sets the false promisor apart is that the lender "cannot possibly concur with my way of acting toward him and hence cannot himself hold the end of this action" (Ak. 429–430). Notice that Kant emphasizes what the lender cannot do instead of what he would not or does not want to do. Different lenders might feel differently about giving a gift rather than a loan if they knew what the borrower was really after. Rather than focusing on the potentially idiosyncratic reactions of lenders, Kant is drawing attention to a feature of the situation that he claims precludes the possibility of concurring with this way of being treated. What is it about the false promisor's action that precludes this possibility? In what follows, I consider two potential interpretations. Although both interpretations suggest some seemingly problematic implications for Kant's view, both also illuminate powerful moral objections to the false promisor's maxim.

The first interpretation draws on the Formula of Universal Law's verdict in the case of the false promise to explain how a false promise precludes the possibility of its recipient concurring with this way of being treated.[3] Recall that the basic moral mistake identified by the Formula of Universal Law is making an exception for oneself. The false promisor attempts to make an exception for himself because the maxim on which he acts cannot be a universal law. If everyone in need of money attempted to make a false promise to obtain it, promises of this kind would not be believed. Thus, the success of the false promise relies on others acting differently. Since the maxim on which the false promisor acts cannot be a universal law, the recipient of the false promise cannot rationally concur with this way of being treated. In this

---

3. Korsgaard, "Kant's Formula of Humanity," 126–27.

way, whenever one's maxim cannot be a universal law, one treats others merely as a means. They are treated in a way that it is impossible for them to accept as rational beings.

A strength of this interpretation of what is involved in treating others merely as a means is that it clarifies how the Formula of Universal Law and the Formula of Humanity are, at bottom, the same principle. While the Formula of Universal Law directs us to the form our maxims must have, requiring that they have the form of a universal law requires us to constrain our actions in light of the others' rational nature, that is, their capacity to set ends for themselves. While the Formula of Humanity directs our attention to the value that rational beings have in themselves, responding appropriately to this value requires adopting maxims that have the form of a universal law. In this way, we may see the Formula of Universal Law and the Formula of Humanity as two sides of the same principle.

A weakness of this interpretation is that it fails to capture the intuitively problematic relationship that seems to exist specifically between the false promisor and the recipient of the false promise. On the interpretation we are considering, no one can concur with the false promisor's maxim because it is not universalizable. That suggests that the false promisor's action treats all other rational beings merely as a means. He makes an exception of himself with respect to all of them. But there seems to be a clear sense in which the recipient of the false promise is wronged in a way that others are not. The above interpretation provides no resources for explaining this.

The second interpretation of what precludes the possibility of concurring with the false promisor's maxim is better able to capture the problematic relationship specifically between the false promisor and the recipient of the false promise. This interpretation holds that the problem with the false promisor's maxim is that the recipient is necessarily denied an opportunity to decide for herself whether or not she will participate in furthering the false promisor's true end, namely taking the money without repaying.[4] For the false promise to be successful, the recipient must remain unaware of its true nature. If she knew that the false promisor intended to keep the money, she might or might not agree to hand it over as a gift rather than a loan. But the false promisor gives her no chance to decide this for herself. The recipient cannot possibly concur with the false promisor's maxim because she cannot know his true end. The false promisor thus treats her merely as a means in a distinctive way.

Although this interpretation can explain how the false promisor wrongs the recipient of the false promise in particular, it faces two other difficulties. First, this interpretation leaves the relationship between the Formula of Universal Law and the Formula of Humanity somewhat obscure. It is not obvious that maxims that deny others the opportunity to decide whether they will contribute to an end will always be maxims that involve making an exception for oneself, and vice versa. For example, if I lie to you in order to get you to a surprise party in your honor, I deny you the opportunity to decide for yourself whether you want to go. But it might well be that everyone could have the maxim of lying to guests of honor about surprise parties without undermining the efficacy of such lies, and hence that such a maxim could have the form of a universal law. In other words, such a maxim does not seem to involve making an exception for oneself. In this way, the duties that follow from the Formula of Universal Law might differ from those that follow from the

---

4. Christine M. Korsgaard, "The Right to Lie: Kant on Dealing with Evil," chap. 5, in *Creating the Kingdom of Ends* (Cambridge: Cambridge University Press, 1996), 138–40.

Formula of Humanity on this second interpretation. This would cast doubt on Kant's claim that they are two formulations of a single categorical imperative.

The surprise party example also reveals the second problem with the second interpretation of what precludes the possibility of concurring with the false promisor's maxim. That interpretation condemns lying for any purpose. Although Kant at times seems to endorse an absolute prohibition on lying, many people take the moral prohibition on lying to be finer-grained. This suggests a tension between the implications of the Formula of Humanity on this interpretation and commonsense morality. Moreover, this interpretation suggests an absolute prohibition on other act types, like force and coercion, which also seem to deny those they are used against the opportunity to decide for themselves whether to contribute to a given end.[5] But in his later work, *The Metaphysics of Morals*, Kant explicitly endorses some permissible instances of force and coercion in order to enforce the laws of a just state. So this interpretation also suggests a tension within Kant's view about the permissibility of these activities.

We have considered two interpretations of what precludes the possibility of concurring with the false promisor's maxim, and hence how that maxim treats the recipient of the false promise merely as a means. Both interpretations analyze the case of the false promise in revealing ways. The first interpretation highlights how making an exception for oneself involves disrespecting others. The second interpretation highlights the disrespect involved in certain ways of manipulating others for one's own purposes. Nonetheless, both interpretations also struggle to explain all that we might want to explain about the morality of this action and others like it. This suggests room for more thinking about how

---

5. Korsgaard, "The Right to Lie," 139–40.

this part of Kant's view should be interpreted and whether Kant's view needs revision.

We have considered Kant's discussion of two perfect duties, a perfect duty to oneself not to kill oneself in order to escape from difficult situations and a perfect duty to others not to make false promises. We will now consider Kant's discussion of two imperfect duties, an imperfect duty to oneself to develop one's own talents and an imperfect duty to others to promote their happiness (Ak. 430). Kant suggests that failing to perform imperfect duties does not involve treating ourselves or others merely as a means. Instead, failing to perform these duties involves failing to "harmonize" with the end of rational nature. Let us consider what this means in each of the examples he gives in turn.

Kant motivates the imperfect duty to develop one's talents as follows: "To neglect these capacities might perhaps be consistent with the maintenance of humanity as an end in itself, but would not be consistent with the advancement of this end" (Ak. 430). How should we square this claim with Kant's claim that we are to relate to humanity, or rational nature, as an end only negatively? Kant seems to envision harmonizing with the end of rational nature as recognizing that this end can give us reasons to act that are not reasons to bring more rational beings into existence. Instead, recognizing the value of one's own rationality gives one reason to develop the capacities through which one expresses one's rationality, that is, the capacities that one utilizes in setting and pursuing ends. One does this by aiming at the development and, indeed, perfection of one's talents.

As I noted above, imperfect duties are duties to pursue a certain end but involve flexibility about the specific actions undertaken in service of that end. We have considerable leeway about how to pursue the end of developing our own talents. Should you pursue this end via violin lessons or via learning a new language?

The discretion we have when fulfilling our imperfect duties is bounded by our perfect duties. Making a false promise to secure violin lessons is not an acceptable way of pursuing the end of developing one's own talents. But beyond this, much will depend on your individual dispositions. If violin lessons bring you joy and you find language lessons tedious, furthering your own happiness will speak in favor of violin lessons. As we are about to see, however, developing our own talents is not the only end we are required to pursue. Kant also argues that we are required to have the end of others' happiness. Our choices about how to develop our talents may also be influenced by this end.

Kant motivates the imperfect duty to promote others' happiness as follows: "the ends of any subject who is an end in himself must as far as possible be my ends also, if that conception of an end in itself is to have its full effect on me" (Ak. 430). Recognizing your value as a fellow rational agent involves recognizing as valuable the ends you set by exercising your rational capacities. Here again, we have some discretion about how best to contribute to others' ends and how to pursue our own ends along with theirs. But furthering the ends of others, and hence their happiness, must be an end for us.

Kant's Formula of Humanity directs us to treat ourselves and our fellow rational beings as ends in ourselves. We have now seen how Kant derives both perfect and imperfect duties to ourselves and others from this principle. Although these derivations leave some matters unsettled, the Formula of Humanity remains a powerful and illuminating way to characterize how morality requires us to treat ourselves and others.

FREEDOM

Lucy Allais

The main passages relevant to Freedom in the *Groundwork* can be found in the following sections: Ak. 446–463.

---

1. Introduction

Freedom is the central topic of the third section of Kant's *Groundwork for the Metaphysics of Morals.* That there is a connection between free will and morality is not an unusual idea: much philosophical writing on the question of freedom of the will is specifically focused on it as the capacity required for our actions to be attributable to us such that it is appropriate and fair to hold us morally responsible for them—to praise and blame us for them. Kant clearly shares the common idea that freedom is bound up with the possibility of moral responsibility. But his account also seems to link freedom and morality more closely in ways that are not easy to understand. Readers trying to untangle *Groundwork*

III might ask some of the questions this essay discusses: How does Kant understand what freedom is? How does his account relate to the traditional free will problem? What is the relation between freedom and autonomy in his account? What role does freedom play in the argument of *Groundwork III*—what does Kant take himself to actually prove in this final section? Among the challenging and frustrating features of the *Groundwork* is the difficulty not only of understanding *how* the argument is supposed to work, but even of working out *what* Kant takes himself to be arguing *for* at each stage. This essay presents an account of these questions. Apart from noting one interpretative controversy at the end, I will mostly just present my reading of Kant. Given the degree to which interpreting Kant is controversial, this means that almost everything I say will be something some other scholar has contested.

2. The will

Kant opens *Groundwork III* asserting that the will is a causal capacity of rational living beings[1] (Ak. 446). Here we have the

---

1. Kant presents his argument in the *Groundwork* as applying to all rational beings, which means it has a wider scope than humans (allowing for the possibility of other rational embodied natural beings, as well as the possibility of disembodied rational beings such as angels and God). Whether it also has a narrower scope than all humans—in other words, whether Kant intends it to apply to all mature humans—is debated, given his racist views about the capacities of some human groups and his sexist views of women, which might be taken to cast doubt on whether he takes these groups to have reason. While this is an important question and key to understanding Kant's thought, the text of the *Groundwork*, on its own, does not say anything to exclude certain humans. Kant does make a racist comment about the Pacific Islanders who he thinks fail to develop their talents, but the comment does not imply that they lack rational capacities. In this paper, I will develop an understanding of Kant's ideas as applying

idea of a causal capacity involved in action and also understood as connected to having reason. Kant has introduced this idea in the previous sections of the text, describing will as practical reason (Ak. 412–413) and saying that the will is a capacity to determine itself to action in conformity with the representation of certain laws, which is a capacity of rational beings (Ak. 427). Although Kant's presentation can make these claims seem a bit strange, we can understand his ideas in relatively familiar ways. The free will problem is centrally about action; willing is a capacity we exercise when we act. Free action—action for which we are appropriately held responsible—is commonly linked with having the rational capacities required to recognize and act on normative requirements or reasons for acting. We don't hold creatures that lack rational capacities (e.g., animals, very young children) morally responsible for their actions. And demonstrating that someone acted with diminished rational capacities is a central way we show that it is not appropriate to hold them responsible for something they did. Kant's talk of understanding this causal capacity in terms of the *representation* of certain laws can be seen as the idea that the *rational capacity* to recognize normative requirements is a cognitive capacity—it concerns requirements we characterize and recognize at the level of thought or mental representation. We will now look at what it would mean for this capacity to be free.

3. Freedom of the will, characterized negatively

Starting with the idea of the will as a causality involving rational capacities in action, or practical rational capacities, Kant then

---

to all humans. Whether or not Kant intended it in this way, and if he did not, what follows from this for how we should understand his ideas, are important questions but are simply beyond the scope of this short piece.

claims that this causality is free when it is efficient independent
of causes outside of itself (Ak. 446). What we mean by a cause
being *efficient* is its bringing something about. Kant says that
freedom would be the property of this causality by which it is the
source or initiation of actions itself rather than being determined
by causes outside of it. When we attribute an action to an agent
in the way that is involved in holding them morally responsible
(appropriately subject to praise or blame), we regard the action
as originating in them—in their will—rather than some causal
force outside them. For example, if you bumped into me because
the wind blew you over, what happened originated in something
outside of you rather than in your will, and I shouldn't hold you
responsible for it. If, in contrast, I think that you freely decided to
push me over, I view the action as, in some sense, originating in
you and not some cause outside of you. Kant calls this a negative
understanding of the causality of freedom. It is negative because
it gives an account of attributing action to a causal capacity of the
agent by saying what the action is *not* caused by—the action is
not determined by something outside of the agent.

Kant's argument in the *Groundwork* draws on, without fully
explaining, an account he develops in his important *Critique of
Pure Reason*, the first edition of which was published four years
before the *Groundwork*, and the second edition, two years after
the *Groundwork*. In this work, Kant presents the problem of
freedom of the will from the point of view he calls theoretical
knowledge or theoretical reason, which is concerned with characterizing the way the world is, as opposed to practical knowledge or practical reason, which is concerned with what we ought
to do. He divides theoretical knowledge into empirical (science)
and non-empirical (metaphysics) accounts of the way the world
is and understands the free will problem as part of metaphysics. He presents the free will problem as a conflict between two

different kinds of causality: the causality of nature and the causality of freedom. Kant holds that when we understand something in terms of the causality of nature, we understand it as determined by some previous state of the world, in accordance with a law of nature. Further, the same understanding applies to the cause of the cause, so this involves thinking of causal chains governed by laws of nature, going backward indefinitely. In the *Groundwork*, he refers to this idea as "natural necessity"—the idea that things have causes that fall under laws of nature and necessitate what happened. In contrast, he claims that the causality of freedom would involve a causal *spontaneity*, or a causality starting a new chain of appearances *from itself* (A 446/B 474; A 533/B 561). Again, Kant characterizes this causality negatively: he explains its beginning something itself by saying it is *not* determined by something that precedes it. He holds further that we can demonstrate that every event that happens in space and time falls under the causality of nature and that empirical knowledge of the world would not be possible if this were not the case. From the point of view of empirical knowledge, explaining why something happened involves appealing to a previous state of the world. For example, we explain how a fire started by describing the conditions (the dryness of the grass) and something that happened (a lightning strike), and we explain these conditions and the thing that happened in terms of previous states of the world and previous things that have happened (a drought, a buildup of atmospheric pressure), and so on.

4. The free will problem

This account of these two kinds of causality generates a version of the traditional problem of free will, which Kant puts as follows: if the causality of nature is *complete*, the causality of freedom would be *impossible*. Suppose everything that happens has a complete causal history tracing indefinitely backward. In that case, there is no space for some of the things that happen (our actions) having a cause that starts in the agent themself and *not* things outside them. And if our actions trace to causes that go back before our existence, it is hard to see how we can be responsible, and liable for praise or blame, for anything we do. We are not responsible for things that happened before we existed, and it does not seem fair to praise or blame us for them. For example, we thought there was a contrast between the wind blowing you into me and your choosing to push me, but if your choosing to push me was also, in fact, something that followed from previous states of the world, including ones that precede your existence, it becomes harder to see how I can hold you responsible for it, and how I can locate its origin in your choice.

Our empirical explanations of things as happening always appeal to a cause that preceded the thing that happened. Whatever else we may be, we are physically embodied creatures. Whatever is true of causal explanations that apply to matter must be true of the matter that makes up our bodies. Things that happen to the matter in our bodies must have causes in the world that precede the thing that happens. It seems to follow from this that with respect to anything that happens to our bodies, a causal history will be traceable backward to something that preceded our choices and even our existence. But if everything that happens to the matter in our bodies can be traced to causes that ultimately precede our existence, it is hard to see how we can be held responsible for our actions. It seems that the way we think about causal explanations in our empirical knowledge of the world is in tension with attributing things we do to our choices.

In the *Groundwork*, Kant presents the idea of "natural necessity" (Ak. 446–447) as saying that everything that happens is determined according to laws of nature or has a preceding cause falling under natural laws and that this conflicts with freedom.

He presents the conflict in terms of the idea (which also features in the *Critique*) that thinking of an action as freely done involves thinking that we could have not done it (Ak. 453). In contrast, natural necessity does not seem to leave space for this possibility (Ak. 455). If you bumped into me because the wind blew you in such a way that it was not possible for you to avoid bumping into me (you couldn't have made anything else happen), you didn't bump into me as a result of your free choice, and I shouldn't blame you for it. When I blame you for it, I think it was possible for you not to do it, but you chose to do it anyway.

Kant says that the conflict between freedom and natural necessity arises from the point of view of theoretical reason. While he thinks we cannot fully understand or resolve the problem, as in the first *Critique*, he allocates to theoretical reason the task of showing that there is, in fact, no contradiction between the causality of nature and the causality of freedom (Ak. 456–457). And as in the *Critique*, this involves appealing to a contrast between the world of sense or experience (the world as it appears to us) and the world of understanding (the world as it is in itself). In the *Critique*, he argues that this contrast enables us to show that the causality of freedom is not impossible because the causality of nature is not complete. It applies only to things as they appear to us, but this does not (and in principle, cannot) exhaust the nature of reality. So the way we think about the world in science, and the metaphysics needed to support science, cannot show the causality of freedom to be impossible. Before looking at this appeal in more detail, we must turn to the relation between freedom and autonomy.

5. Freedom of the will, characterized positively

So far, we have given a negative account of what it would be for the will, as a causality of rational beings, to be free: its bringing about action (its being an efficient cause) must *not* be determined by something outside of or alien to it. This does not, however, give us an account of how free action *is* caused or what it is for an action to originate in or be attributable to an agent. In the contemporary free will debate, it is often pointed out that to say that an action is *not* determined by previous states of the world does not give us any account of how an agent is accountable for it. Not being causally determined seems, for example, compatible with simply randomly occurring, and an action's occurring randomly does not seem to locate its origin in an agent's will in the way that makes them accountable for it. Suppose your pushing me was the result of a truly random quantum fluctuation in your brain. In this case, while it may be true that the cause is not (like the wind) something outside of you, it seems no more reasonable to hold you responsible for random quantum fluctuations than for the wind. Kant says that unless a free will is governed by or determined by *something* it would be an absurdity (Ak. 446, rational capacities in action could not be randomness), but if it were determined by something outside of itself, it would not be free. He then gives a positive account of what it is for an action to originate in an agent in terms of the idea that the agent's action involves a causal capacity that is governed by a law that comes from itself—from reason.

By this stage of the work, Kant has already presented and argued for an account of the principle that comes from reason itself: the categorical imperative, which he also takes to give an account of the will's autonomy. The will's autonomy is its being governed by a law that comes from reason itself: this makes it self-governed, which is what autonomy is. If practical reason— working out what we ought to do—were an inner capacity of agents but one directed toward or in the service of something outside of the will or reason, such as happiness, it would not involve acting under a requirement that comes *from reason*. One might think of an animal as, in some sense, acting from inner principles (animals have perception and desires), but these are in the service of, or directed by, instinct or laws of its nature and not its free choice. Kant argues that the only principle that comes from reason is his categorical imperative, which, in previous sections, he has presented as telling us to take rational agents as providing a constraint or limit on what counts as a reason for acting ("that the rational being itself is the supreme limiting condition in all use of means," Ak. 438), which he also says is the same as requiring the principles of our action to be universally valid.

To understand this account of freedom, we need not worry about the exact details of these formulations of the categorical imperative. Suppose Kant were right that reason must be governed by a higher-order rational commitment not grounded in anything other than reason. In that case, this could be an account of reason's autonomy, independently of what the best way of characterizing this higher-order principle turns out to be. Kant's idea seems to be that because reason's being governed by a principle that comes only from reason itself is its autonomy, it gives us a positive characterization of freedom. It gives us a way of understanding what it is to locate an action in the agent themself: this is a matter of seeing the action originating in a causal capacity governed by a commitment to a normative requirement that comes from the agent themself—from their practical rational capacities.

The negative characterization of freedom is metaphysical: it involves seeing an action as not determined by previous states of the world in accordance with natural necessity or laws of nature. In contrast, the positive characterization is not metaphysical but appeals to normative considerations: the idea of rational capacities in action as governed by a higher-order rational commitment, that of regarding the humanity of each person as a constraint on what counts as a reason for action. Showing that the negative characterization is not ruled out—is not impossible—is the task of theoretical reason. Giving a positive metaphysical or theoretical characterization of what it is for an action to originate in the agent is something Kant thinks is not possible for us, but a positive characterization can be given at the level of practical reason. For an action to originate in us is for it to flow from *our* practical rational abilities, and for these abilities to be ours is for them not to be subject to something outside of themselves (something outside of practical reason) but rather to be governed by something that comes from reason itself, its governing normative commitment. So it seems that, on Kant's account, freedom of the will is characterized partly metaphysically and partly by normative considerations.

6. But can we freely do wrong?

Kant famously states that a free will and a will under moral laws are the same (Ak. 447) and that autonomy of the will is a matter of being governed by or acting under the moral law. This might make it seem as if we are free only when we do as morality requires: when we act on the principle that comes from reason itself. The obvious problem with this is that it would make our actions free only when they are morally motivated, which would make our immoral actions not free, meaning it would not be appropriate to hold us responsible for them. Reading Kant in this way would attribute to him a very implausible position, and one that he does not hold, since he clearly does hold us responsible for our immoral actions. This means we need an explanation of what it is to act under a rational principle and to be determined by rational requirements, which is not the same as always acting as this principle says we should. Kant holds that our actions are free and imputable when they originate in a causality that is not determined by natural necessity, and also we act "under" or governed by a commitment to reason's principle. Being governed by or acting under a principle need not mean only doing what it requires: it is possible to act against a principle you are committed to.

Kant's account of acting under a principle can be taken to mean that we are validly subject to it (it applies to us) and that we are committed to it in the sense that we recognize it as applying to us, and where this commitment is not a choice or optional but is part of what it is to have reason. Consider, as an (imperfect) analogy, reasoning under a commitment to the principle of non-contradiction: any statement of the form *p and not-p* must be false. Unless we are validly subject to this principle (it applies to us) and we *take* ourselves to be reasoning under it (we recognize, at least implicitly, it as applying), what we are doing isn't really *reasoning*. Similarly, on Kant's account, when we exercise practical rational capacities (when we act), we have a causal capacity that we exercise under a commitment to reason's governing principle: we are validly subject to the principle, and we are committed to it. This means that whenever we act wrongly, we act against a principle we are committed to, and indeed one we see as being unconditionally valid for us. Kant thinks, therefore, that when, for example, a shopkeeper cheats their customers for profit, they know that they should not do this, and they are, in fact (at some level), committed to a principle that says that they should not do it.

While Kant's claim that morality is bound up with autonomy of the will makes it sound as if acting freely or autonomously is acting morally, note that he does not talk of acting *autonomously*, but instead of the *autonomy of the will* and the *principle* of autonomy. Suppose we (in contemporary terms) think of acting autonomously (not Kant's term) as acting freely. Then Kant's account says that we act autonomously both when we act as the principle of autonomy requires and when we act against it, so long as we have the requisite rational and causal capacities to act *under* it. When we have these capacities, our will has the property of autonomy, even if we act against the principle of autonomy, because our will is governed by the principle, committed to it, and validly subject to it. When our will has the property of autonomy, and we act with the causality of freedom, our actions are free, and we can be held responsible for them.

7. The argument of Section III

Having some sense of the ideas Kant is appealing to in this section, we can now try to put them together to see what he actually argues with them. That practical rational abilities, or rational abilities in action, are central to the freedom needed for moral responsibility is a relatively standard view. Kant adds to this a very specific characterization of what it is to have practical rational abilities, in terms of a specific, unconditional commitment, expressed in the categorical imperative. In the previous parts of the *Groundwork*, Kant argued that his account of reason's principle follows analytically from the notion of morality (Ak. 440). We have not considered these arguments here. I take him, roughly, to say that since morality is characterized by unconditional reasons for action or normative requirements, such reasons can be grounded only in something that is an end in itself, and must have a universalizable form. But this does not show that our wills *are* such that they are bound by this principle; it just shows that *if* there are moral reasons, this principle gives an account of their form. He now asserts that *if* we assume that our wills are free, morality follows because autonomy of the will is both what it is for the will to be free and the moral law (reason's highest principle). The unconditional principle that gives the form of the moral law is the only principle that comes from reason itself. So it is the only way we can positively characterize action as originating in an agent's rational capacities.

But are we entitled to assume that we are free? Kant now argues that every being that cannot act except under the idea of freedom really is free in a practical respect (Ak. 448). This is not just an account of a pragmatic assumption. Rather, the idea is that we cannot think of ourselves as acting without thinking of ourselves as acting for reasons (rational requirements or normative considerations), and in recognizing normative requirements, Kant thinks we are committed to reason's principle. But if we act under reason's principle, the positive (practical) characterization of what it is for an action to originate in us applies to us—this is what it is to be free. We cannot think of someone as acting for reasons (or out of recognition of normative requirements) and not think of them in this way (Ak. 448). From the point of view of practical reason, then, we have all the grounds we need for thinking of ourselves and each other as free.

However, it would be a problem if freedom could be demonstrated to be impossible on theoretical grounds; this is why the limited result of theoretical reason—that freedom is not impossible—is crucial. Further, the perspective from which theoretical reason shows this, Kant says, is not an obscure philosophical account but is central to the way we all think of ourselves. We think of ourselves from the perspective or standpoint of empirical causal explanation. But we also think of ourselves from the very different perspective of normative requirements, which empirical causal explanations cannot capture. This means we are committed to understanding empirical causal explanations as incomplete—as not explaining everything. But if empirical causal explanation is incomplete, the causality of freedom is not impossible: Kant holds that this is all we can show from theoretical reason or metaphysics—but also all we need to show. The way we are committed to thinking of ourselves when we act is an unavoidable part of how we think about ourselves, and it is also legitimate, because science or metaphysics does not rule it out.

A central controversy in understanding Kant's account is how to understand his appeal to the contrast between the worlds of sense and understanding. On one way of reading it, the idea is that once the two standpoints—empirical or scientific, causal explanation on the one hand, and normative explanation on the other—are properly understood as the completely different orders of explanation they are, we will realize that they don't operate in the same spheres and so are in no danger of conflicting. This would mean that the completeness of metaphysical determinism (natural necessity) in its own sphere of explanation would no longer be seen as a threat to freedom. This reading sees Kant's account as not unlike some versions of what are now called *compatibilist* accounts of freedom of the will: accounts of free will that see it as compatible with the position of metaphysical determinism, which states that everything that happens is determined by previous states of the world, so at any given time only one future is possible, and it is never true that anyone could have acted differently than they actually did. On this reading, explanations of action involving our reasons are such a completely different kind of explanation that there simply is no danger of conflict.

An alternative (which is my view) appeals to the fact that Kant's account of free agency involves an efficient causality that is *not* determined by causes external to it, so he has a version of what is now called an incompatibilist account of freedom of the will, the position that freedom is possible only if everything that happens is not set by the initial state of the universe and the laws of nature. Practical reason is, after all, not simply mapping an account of what ought to happen but is about initiating *action*. On this account, Kant's resolution of the free will problem needs to show that "natural necessity" is incomplete. He does this by showing that metaphysical determinism (the universality of natural necessity) is not a claim within science but rather goes beyond what we could possibly have grounds for asserting from the point of view of empirical (scientific) knowledge. This shows that science cannot rule out the causality of freedom, which is all we need to show from the perspective of theoretical reason.

As I understand Kant's account, he holds that we have a causal capacity that we cannot characterize metaphysically apart from saying that it involves not being determined by previous states of the world, which science cannot rule out, and which we exercise when we act under a commitment to normative requirements we are validly subject to, which is what it is to have practical rational abilities in action. This account can seem complex and strange, but the idea that we have a causal capacity to act governed by rational requirements is central to our ordinary thinking of rational capacities as requisite for holding people responsible. And when we hold people (and ourselves) responsible, we typically think that they (and we) could have acted differently. We do not characterize what they did in terms of a previous state of the world that caused something to happen but in terms of their reasons or the principles on which they acted.

About the Contributors

Lucy Allais is Professor of Philosophy at Johns Hopkins University and the University of the Witwatersrand, Johannesburg.

Anne Margaret Baxley is Associate Professor of Philosophy at Washington University in St. Louis.

Steven M. Cahn is Professor Emeritus of Philosophy at the City University of New York Graduate Center.

Kyla Ebels-Duggan is Professor of Philosophy at Northwestern University.

Nataliya Palatnik is Assistant Professor of Philosophy at the University of Wisconsin—Milwaukee.

Japa Pallikkathayil is Associate Professor of Philosophy at the University of Pittsburgh.

Laura Papish is Associate Professor of Philosophy at George Washington University.

Tamar Schapiro is Professor of Philosophy at the Massachusetts Institute of Technology.

Index

actions: and autonomy, 86–88; causality of, 82; consequences of, 8–9, 30; contradiction in principles of, 54–55; done from duty, 11–15, 25, 28–31, 38–39; done from inclination, 13–15, 38; done in accord with duty, 11–14, 28–29; and free will, 81, 85–86; and gifts of fortune, 3–4; and gifts of nature, 3; and good will, 1–2, 6–12; maxim of, 14, 51–53; and moral good, 2, 13–15, 30, 37; moral motivations for, 45–46; moral worth of, 2, 12–14, 23, 29–30, 37; and natural necessity, 84–85; nature of, 67; and practical reason, 86–91; and rational principles, 88–89; reasons for, 35; responsibility for, 84–85; and universal law, 15, 48; and utilitarianism, 61

autonomy: and categorical imperative, 86; and free action, 86–88; and freedom, 80, 85–91; and morality, 89–90; and reason, 87; of the will, 88–91

categorical imperative: concept of, 38, 41–42, 45–46, 51–52; hypothetical imperative versus, 41–44; and moral motivations, 45–47; and reason, 86–87, 90; as supreme moral principle, 65; unconditional requirements of, 45, 50–51, 66–67; and universal law, 15, 46–48, 50–52, 60, 74–75; and value of actions, 42–44. *See also* Formula of Humanity; Formula of Universal Law

causality: efficient, 82, 86, 92; empirical explanations for, 91–93; of freedom, 82–85, 92–93; and free will problem, 82–83; of nature, 83–85; normative requirements of, 91–93; and physical embodiment, 84; and practical rational capacities, 81–82

law, 27–32, 34; and promo-
tion of happiness in others,
23

self-perfection, 33–34
spontaneity, 83
suicide: and good will, 9; and
one's own happiness, 22,
32; and perfect duty, 34–35,
71–72, 77
supreme principle of morality,
2, 11

theoretical knowledge/reason,
82, 85, 91

unhappiness, 24–25
universalization: of maxims,
28, 52–55, 61; maxims and
contradiction of, 53–55,
57–60; and moral law, 28;
and need for moral judg-
ment, 60–61
universal law: and actions
done from duty, 15; and
categorical imperative,
46–52, 60; formula of,
51–53, 60, 62–63; maxims
of, 15, 45–46, 49, 51–53,

66, 74–75; and the will, 47,
51–53. *See also* Formula of
Universal Law
utilitarianism, 61

value: of good will, 6, 9–10,
20; of happiness, 19–21,
68–69; of inclinations,
68–69; of rational beings,
68–69, 74, 77–78; unconditional, 67–69
virtue, 4, 19–20, 42, 61

will, the: autonomy of, 88–91;
as causal capacity of
rational beings, 80, 80n1,
81–82; corruption of, 5–6;
freedom of, 80–86; and
moral law, 15, 88; and
moral strength, 25; and
practical knowledge/reason,
82; as practical reason, 81;
and theoretical knowledge/
reason, 82, 85; and universal law, 47, 51–53. *See also*
freedom and free will;
good will
World of the Universalized
Maxim, 54–57, 61

Readers' Notes

Readers' Notes

Readers' Notes

Readers' Notes